The Case for Earmarked Taxes

Government Spending and Public Choice

An American Perspective: Theory and an Example

RANJIT S. TEJA

International Monetary Fund

Earmarking in Britain: Theory and Practice

BARRY BRACEWELL-MILNES

Published by
INSTITUTE OF ECONOMIC AFFAIRS
1991

First published in February 1991 by

The Institute of Economic Affairs,
2 Lord North Street,
Westminster, London SW1P 3LB

Research Monograph 46

ISSN 0073-9103

ISBN 0-255 36241-2

*The Institute gratefully acknowledges financial support for its
publications programme and other work from a generous benefaction
by the late Alec and Beryl Warren.*

Printed in Great Britain by
Goron Pro-Print Co. Ltd.,
Churchill Industrial Estate, Lancing, W. Sussex
Filmset in 'Berthold' Univers 9 on 11pt Medium

Contents

Foreword

Academic economists and national ministries of finance have not, in recent years, devoted much attention to the theory or practice of earmarked taxes.

This may be because economists have in the past regarded them as somewhat obvious and rigid instruments, tied to a particular public spending objective, insufficiently flexible to cope with the many and changing spending patterns of the modern welfare state.

Finance ministries in advanced democracies have tended to view them with ill-concealed distaste. A simple link between taxpayer contribution and spending outcome conjures up alarming visions of taxpayers demanding a say in the nature and balance of public spending itself. It is assumed that, were taxpayers to be equipped with more visible means of identifying public spending allocations, chaos would ensue. Defence spending in particular is conjured up as a reason not to investigate the scope for earmarking.

These attitudes may now be changing. Systems of financing public spending that may have been appropriate for stable, high-spending economies may fit less well in an environment of privatisation, contracting-out of public services and economic transition. Nor are existing models of public finance so clearly satisfactory that new options should not be subjected to careful study.

In this *Research Monograph* Ranjit Teja of the International Monetary Fund and Dr Barry Bracewell-Milnes of the Institute make a helpful scholarly contribution towards more informed discussion. Their work starts from the supposition that tax earmarking has a theoretical rationale which ties in closely to the economics of bureaucracy, or public choice. Teja in particular makes it clear that much traditional opposition to earmarking stems from a 'benevolent social planner' approach, whilst a different view of society, that voters with differing preferences attempt to arrive at a consensus to support alternative public expenditure, tends to support earmarking.

They show that identifying taxes with defined parts of public spending can assist in achieving a closer assessment of individual preferences, improve compliance, stabilise revenue flows, and protect valuable public spending areas against less socially productive projects which, in an undifferentiated tax system, may crowd them out.

It is of particular interest to consider the chequered history of earmarking in British taxation. The picture suggests that laudable early intentions have given way to political pressure: so that tax contributions which might understandably be assumed to go towards, for example, road building and maintenance end up in general expenditure; whilst an extended range of social programmes involves apparent earmarking which conceals large transfers from general taxation.

Dr Barry Bracewell-Milnes makes it clear that it will be some time before the long-term shift towards an expenditure tax which he foresees will ease these problems. In the meantime, he insists, earmarking has work to do. He shows how this might apply within income tax, to a specific health tax; and in a reformed system of local government finance where local authority expenditure would be financed entirely by the community charge and the community charge would be earmarked entirely for the financing of local government expenditure. The relationship between an earmarked tax and other methods of financing government expenditure, including direct charging, is also explored.

Those who are engaged in the theory and practice of public finance, budgetary and spending issues will find these ideas timely, and the authors' approach illuminating. Thinking about tax methods and their analogy with charging has tended to lag behind changing economic structures. The firmly market-based economies of the third millennium will require tax systems that are compatible with the greatest possible competition and choice in the provision of services to the public. Whilst the Institute and its Trustees, Advisers and Directors must be dissociated from the analysis and conclusions of the authors of this *Research Monograph*, they are pleased to offer it as an important contribution to informed discussion and debate.

February 1991

GRAHAM MATHER
General Director

PART ONE:

An American Perspective: Theory and an Example

RANJIT S. TEJA

The Author

RANJIT S. TEJA is an economist in the Asian Department of the International Monetary Fund. He holds degrees in mathematics and economics from Delhi University, Jawaharlal Nehru University, and Columbia University, New York. He has published articles on international finance, macro-economics, and famine.

ONE

Introduction

The earmarking of taxes refers to the designation of funds—either from a single tax base or from a wider pool of revenues—to a particular end-use. Typical examples include the earmarking of revenues from property taxes for education, gasoline taxes for highway construction, and payroll taxes for social security payments. This may be contrasted with general fund financing where expenditures are financed from consolidated receipts. Earmarking provisions are a pervasive fiscal phenomenon in both developed and developing economies and are even written into the constitutions of some countries.

For a number of reasons, the practice has been condemned as wasteful and inefficient. At the bottom of much of this criticism is the homely analogy with households constrained to spending the receipts from each source of income for specific items of consumption: which economist has not experienced a twinge of shame when earmarking income from a spouse's new job towards the down-payment on a house, or converting windfall profits into a vacation budget? The source of embarrassment is the knowledge that an earmarking provision is, from the individual's perspective, an unnecessary constraint in the utility-maximisation problem of allocating the last dollar to yield equal marginal utility in every direction. As is argued below, to appreciate the case for earmarked taxes, a necessary first step is to get away from the tendency to view the fiscal problem from the perspective of an individual called the benevolent social planner.

Section 2 of this paper assesses the theoretical case for earmarking and also provides an explanation for its widespread adoption. 'Theoretical' refers to the conventional analyses of welfare economics and public choice theory. These may be distinguished from the 'practical' aspects of public administration and budgeting. Readers from the latter tradition—particularly those familiar with the extreme forms of earmarking found in parts of Latin America and Africa—are apt to receive the arguments in this section with, at best, courteous cynicism. At the risk of some oversimplification, this may be attributed to an underlying tendency to regard the task of budgeting and administration from the point of view of the representative household, or, what amounts to the same thing, from the perspective of the benevolent social planner. This attitude prevents a proper appreciation of what emerges in Section 2 as the true rôle of earmarking in public finance: that of a mechanism for the resolution of differing and conflicting preferences in society. In reading Section 2, it is also important to bear in mind two sets of distinctions:

(a) *normative* versus *positive* analysis; and

(b) arguments supporting earmarking for *specific* expenditures versus arguments supporting full-scale earmarking for *all* public expenditure.

Standard examples of earmarked taxes, such as the gasoline tax earmarked for highway construction or maintenance and the social security tax, have fostered the view that they are basically a means of taxing only those who directly benefit from a certain expenditure. (The obverse of this phenomenon is incredulity at seeing taxes on liquor earmarked for education rather than for the rehabilitation of alcoholics.) It is remarkable, therefore, that the theoretical literature on earmarked taxes deals almost exclusively with 'pure' public goods (that is, characterised by the impossibility or inefficiency of excluding any member of a community once a good has been supplied)—a context in which viewing earmarked taxes as 'benefit taxes' becomes somewhat ambiguous.

The economic rationale and the political motives for earmarking taxes are more subtle than those suggested by the benefits theory of taxation. However, once impure public goods are considered (goods with externalities, local public goods, and so on), the benefits theory of taxation moves centre stage as a normative criterion. In that case an earmarked tax is essentially a user charge and differs only in its mode of collection.

It will thus be most fruitful to classify the theoretical arguments for earmarked taxes according to the public-goods characteristics of the commodity or service in question. Sections 2.1 and 2.2 examine alternative perspectives for dealing with 'pure' public goods; this may be regarded as the 'pure theory of earmarked taxation'. Section 2.3 covers the economics of user charges and the potential choice between earmarking and user charges. The part played by earmarking as a rule-enforcing device is examined in Sections 2.4 and 2.5. Finally, Section 2.6 presents some additional considerations not formally modelled in the literature.

Section 3 briefly examines the case against earmarking from the perspective of efficient budgeting and administration. Section 4 utilises the framework developed in the previous two sections to assess the practice of earmarking in Colombia. The paper concludes in Section 5 with an indication of the circumstances in which earmarking may be recommended.

TWO

The Theoretical Rationale for Earmarked Taxes

1. Lindahl's Theory

Decisions on the provision of public goods may be taken either in the context of a vigorous democracy with an active legislature or, alternatively, by executive decree. Here, we adopt the former perspective and, in this context, begin by disposing of the questionable analogy with the household that earmarks earnings from different sources for various end-uses. This analogy would have been appropriate if it were indeed true that legislatures made decisions the way individuals do. An earmarking provision is then an unnecessary constraint in the utility-maximisation problem of allocating the last dollar to yield equal marginal utility in every direction. But it is a fact of life that a legislature is a forum where *conflicting* preferences are expressed and resolved. Moreover, a legislature, in principle, does not make expenditure decisions without simultaneously determining revenue requirements.

Both these features that distinguish fiscal decision-making from that of the individual household were elegantly captured in the writings of Knut Wicksell and, subsequently, Eric Lindahl over 60 years ago. A by-product of that analysis was a theoretical case for earmarked taxation based on the Pareto criterion of welfare economics, that is, that a situation is Pareto-efficient (or Pareto-optimal) if, and only if, no re-arrangement is possible without inflicting a loss on one or more of the participants. The main point is that the alternative to earmarked taxes—general fund financing—will result in non-Pareto-efficient outcomes.

Lindahl's theory is explained in the Appendix (page 37). In the example cited, the earmarking solution is necessary for Pareto-efficiency: both individuals can be made better off by moving from general fund financing to earmarking.

This case for earmarking has been couched in terms of numbers of equations and unknowns. However, given that the problem is resolved when preferences are identical, it should be clear that the rôle of earmarking lies in facilitating the mutual accommodation of differing preferences in the economy. Moreover, since tax shares are derived from individuals' differing marginal utilities conferred by public goods, the tax shares may be viewed as a form of 'benefits taxation'. Although everyone consumes the same level of public goods, agents pay for this in accordance with their marginal utility (benefit).

Although the Lindahl theory espouses widespread earmarking for each public good, the accounts can always be consolidated once a consensus has been reached. This prevents the myopia that may arise, as a practical matter, when there are a myriad of special funds in the budget. Also, the analysis presumes that agents continually re-assess taxes and expenditures through time.

As students of public economics well know, a fundamental shortcoming of Lindahl's analysis is the assumption that agents in the economy will truthfully reveal their preferences. Equations (3') to (6') in the Appendix state that an individual's tax burden for any particular public good is determined by his marginal rate of substitution *vis-à-vis* private goods. Owing to the non-excludability in consumption inherent in pure public goods, an agent has every incentive to understate the marginal benefit derived from an additional unit of the public good. Although economists have devised clever (and sometimes bizarre) mechanisms for the truthful revelation of preferences that tend towards the Lindahl equilibrium, the implementation of Lindahl's solution remains a complex and difficult issue.[1]

2. The Public Choice Perspective

While a mainstream theorist is apt to view earmarking as a constraint on expenditure, the public choice school stands this proposition on its head and argues, instead, that it is general fund financing that imposes constraints on voters' choices. General fund financing involves the acceptance of a budget that effectively requires consumers to purchase (through payment of taxes) a *bundle* of complex and heterogeneous products. This forces the public to consume goods in a less than optimal mix. As Buchanan has put it, '... any requirement that one stick of butter be purchased with each loaf of bread would surely produce inefficiency in choice ...'.[2] Public choice theory—like Lindahl's

---

[1] For a good review of preference revelation mechanisms, see D. C. Mueller, *Public Choice*, Cambridge University Press, 1979, pp. 68-9.

[2] J. M. Buchanan, 'The Economics of Earmarked Taxes', *Journal of Political Economy*, October 1963, pp. 457-69.

theory—explains the existence of earmarking and draws normative conclusions from its potential rôle in facilitating individual preferences. The main difference lies in the fact that Lindahl's theory is predicated on complete consensus, whereas public choice theory recognises the existence of majority voting.

An important distinction between earmarked taxation and general fund financing can be illustrated as follows. Under the former, the equilibrium quantity of each public good is determined by a separate vote along with a specified tax, or set of taxes, to finance that expenditure. The opportunity cost to the voter of an additional battleship is then higher taxes rather than reduced expenditure on other public goods. General fund financing, on the other hand, is characterised by separate voting on the *size* of the budget (tax bills) and the *composition* of expenditures (expenditure bills). Given the government's separately determined budget constraint, the opportunity cost of an extra battleship is no longer higher taxes but instead reduced expenditure on other public goods. This separation of tax decisions and expenditure decisions lies at the heart of the public choice school's normative case for earmarked taxes.

One strand of this approach—initiated in Buchanan's seminal paper[1]—argues that the voter who might have approved a tax increase if it were earmarked to, say, environmental protection would oppose it under general fund financing because he or she may expect the increment to be allocated to an unfavoured expenditure such as defence. Earmarked taxation then permits a more satisfactory expression of individual preferences. While Buchanan's analysis is basically an exercise in positive economics, it has distinct normative overtones.

A second strand—developed in Browning[2]—draws attention to the possibility of perverse outcomes under general fund financing that may argue for the institution of widespread earmarking. The constraints imposed by the separation of tax decisions and expenditure decisions are sufficiently serious that there is little basis for predicting the outcome under general fund financing. It may well turn out that a lower quantity of a public good will be supplied even if every voter's preference for that good increases.

---

[1] J. M. Buchanan, *op. cit.*

[2] E. K. Browning, 'Collective Choice and General Fund Financing', *Journal of Political Economy*, October 1975.

Budget size and composition under earmarking and general fund financing

Both these points can be demonstrated using a simple model developed by Browning.[1] Consider a community of three voters (A, B and C) consuming two public goods (G and S) and a composite private good (X). Each agent (A, B and C) maximises his utility subject to the budget constraint that his income is the sum of his expenditure on X and his tax contributions towards G and S.

How is the budget decided under earmarking? Assume that voter A is the median voter on the issues of how much of both G and S are to be supplied to the public.[2] Under simple majority voting, the decisions on G and S are made separately, say, first G and then S. A will immediately gravitate to the point of his preferred expenditure pattern and in so doing will implicitly accede to being taxed first by an amount sufficient to support his preferred amounts of G and S. This is precisely what is referred to as 'earmarking': the practice of taking a decision on each public good, together with a decision on taxes to finance that expenditure, separately from other public goods.

How are the size and the composition of the budget decided upon under general fund financing? The *size* of the budget is the value of G plus S. Consideration of a sequence of budget sizes yields, for each agent, the preferred *composition* of the budget for every budget size.

If A is assumed to have the median preference as regards both budget composition and budget size, then in this special case, the general fund financing and earmarking solutions are identical. On the other hand, if A has the median preference with regard to budget *mix* but B has the median preference for budget *size*, then the general fund financing solution is dominated by A's preferences on budget composition.

Welfare effects

With these preliminaries in hand, we can now turn to the point raised by Buchanan.[3] Buchanan compared earmarking with the case where an exogenous 'budgetary authority' sets the budget mix while voters can choose only the size of the budget. If voter A

---

[1] The proofs of Browning's arguments are given in IMF Working Paper 88/18.

[2] Note that the three voters' optima are such that, relatively to A, C prefers more S, while B prefers less S. This makes A the median voter on the amount of S to be supplied. Likewise, A is also the median voter on the equilibrium quantity of G.

[3] J. M. Buchanan, *op. cit.*

17

happens to be the median voter on the size of the budget, the bureaucracy's choice will definitely lower A's welfare, since A is the median voter on the issues of both budget size and budget mix. It is also possible that the bureaucracy's choice will lower *everyone's* welfare.

While the condemnation of general fund financing is stark in this instance, the result is obviously not general. In particular, it is arbitrary to assume an exogenous selection of the budget mix (or, alternatively, of the size of the budget). As we have already seen, public choice under general fund financing can be generalised to an endogenous selection of both budget size and budget mix—in other words, selection of both through voter preferences. Whenever one voter does not possess the median preference on the issue of both budget composition and budget size (in other words, when the earmarking and general fund financing solutions are different), then at least one of the parties will be made worse off by a move to earmarking.

Both earmarking and general fund financing are *constrained* Pareto-efficient (constrained by given tax shares; *Pareto-efficient* means that any alteration would make at least one person worse off). The moral is that the choice between earmarking and general fund financing ultimately depends on the preferred concept of social welfare, and there are no easy generalisations. The analysis is thus useful for predicting support for earmarking provisions but not for drawing normative conclusions.

Perverse outcomes under general fund financing

Turning now to Browning's point about perverse outcomes under general fund financing, suppose that, starting from an equilibrium position, all three voters' preference for G increases. Although A remains the median voter on budget composition, A rather than B now determines the actual size of the budget. It is possible for the new equilibrium amount of G publicly supplied to fall, despite a unanimous increase in preference for G—a paradoxical outcome that could not occur under earmarked taxes. The paradox arises from the dependence on the preferences of the median voter. The issues under earmarking and general fund financing are different; under the latter, budget size and budget composition are chosen *separately*. The median voter associated with the distinct issues of budget size and budget composition may change, and this will influence the outcome. No such complication affects decision-making under earmarking.

The public choice analysis is frequently received with scepticism.

Goode,[1] for example, draws attention to its irrelevance in countries that lack provision for citizen participation. A much stronger criticism of its normative aspects—even in circumstances where they may be valid—is the underlying assumption that voters continuously (or even once in a while) re-evaluate their position on earmarking. A widely noted tendency (see, for example, Deran[2]) is for earmarking provisions to become embedded in the state's financial structure and not to be re-evaluated as conditions change. In practice, the level of public goods supplied will depend entirely on the amount of earmarked revenues and costs, regardless of whether that level has become excessive or deficient. While the usual example cited in this regard is unduly horrifying (the continued presence in two US states during the mid-1960s of taxes earmarked for Confederate pensions), most would agree that rigidity in earmarking provisions is the ultimate flaw in the concept. The moral is that such provisions should be mandatorily reviewed at regular intervals.

3. The Benefits Principle of Taxation and the Economics of User Charges

Frequently, the use of earmarked taxation is justified by invoking the 'benefits principle of taxation', which argues that taxes should be borne by those who most benefit from the associated expenditure. The notion is appealing to economists because it parallels the market mechanism for private goods. The analogy makes most sense when an impure public good is characterised by excludability in consumption.[3] Then it becomes possible to finance the activity with a user charge. Although user charges are in a sense 'earmarked' to their associated activity, the implementation of a user charge is not equivalent to an earmarked tax in terms of efficiency and equity. When the implementation of user charges is judged to be administratively infeasible or too costly, an earmarked tax can be used as a *second-best* instrument of finance (for example, a gasoline tax as a *proxy* for charges on highway users). In this case, it is essential that the base of the earmarked tax bears some relation to the level of public consumption.

The simple economics of user charges sheds some light on the

---

[1] R. Goode, *Government Finance in Developing Countries*, Washington DC: The Brookings Institution, 1984, pp. 11-13.

[2] E. Deran, 'Earmarking and Expenditures: A Survey and a New Test', *National Tax Journal*, December 1965.

[3] An example of a pure public good that is not excludable in consumption is street lighting.

Figure 1:
Provision of a Public Good with Positive Externalities

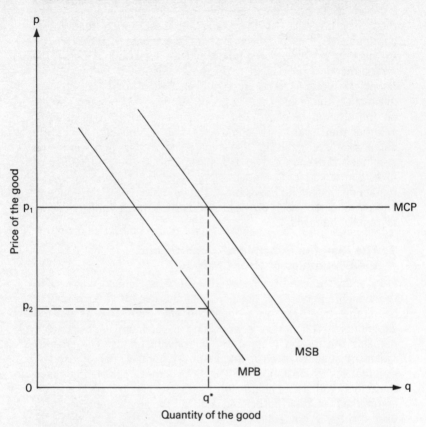

Quantity of the good

principles that determine the extent of revenues to be earmarked. Consider the provision of an excludable public good characterised by *positive externalities*.[1] In Figure 1, the marginal social benefit (MSB) on the vertical axis from a unit of consumption exceeds the corresponding private benefit (MPB). The marginal cost of production (MCP) is, for simplicity, assumed to be constant at p_1. The optimal level of consumption for society is q^*, for which consumers are willing to pay only p_2. Then q^* can be publicly provided by a user charge of p_2, together with a per unit subsidy of

---

[1] *Positive externalities* are benefits to the general public additional to the benefits for which users can be charged. Thus, an excludable public good characterised by positive externalities is a partially excludable public good.

$(p_1 - p_2)$. The subsidy will have to come from the government's general fund rather than from direct consumers. Financing should come entirely from general funds only if social benefits are so large as to imply a user charge so low that it would barely cover the added costs of collection.

It is possible that, owing to price distortions in the economy, the financial cost of implementing user charges may diverge from the social opportunity cost of employing these resources elsewhere: in practice, the opportunity cost of using experienced managers and accountants may be extremely high in developing countries. It may make sense in such a circumstance to earmark revenues from an easily administered tax base that varies positively with the level of public good consumption, for example, gasoline tax revenues for highway construction and maintenance. Ideally, earmarked revenues should total $p_2 q^*$, while the remainder, $(p_1 - p_2)q^*$, is financed by general revenues unrelated to the level of consumption of the good. In practice, this is precisely how expenditure on road construction and maintenance is financed in a number of countries. Eklund[1] reports that, for a cross-section of countries with earmarking provisions, an average of 63 per cent of all road expenditure was financed out of the general fund.

4. Bureaucracy versus the Legislature

A somewhat more institutionalist perspective on earmarking may be gained by pursuing in greater detail—as Niskanen[2] has done—the question of who precisely supplies public goods and services. While demand for public goods is expressed and resolved in the legislature, public goods are generally supplied by bureaucracies. According to one view, the distinguishing characteristic of a bureaucracy is the absence of external control on efficiency and weak internal incentives. Weak external control results from the ambiguous nature of a bureaucracy's output[3] and the dependence of the legislature on the bureaucracy for information. Weak internal incentives to produce efficiently are a consequence of an absence of financial incentives for managers and a lack of competition in the market for their final output. The

---

[1] P. Eklund, 'A Theory of Earmarking Appraised', *National Tax Journal*, June 1972.

[2] W. A. Niskanen, Jr., *Bureaucracy and Representative Government*, Chicago: Aldine Atherton, 1971; also Niskanen, *Bureaucracy: Servant or Master?*, Hobart Paperback No. 5, London: Institute of Economic Affairs, 1973.

[3] For example, the Ministry of Defence produces an amalgam of soldiers, guns, ships and aircraft from which the final output of interest to the consumer—defence services—must be inferred.

effect of this constellation of circumstances is to make bureaucrats pursue goals other than efficiency, such as larger staff establishments, prestige and patronage. As most of these are positively related to the size of the budget, Niskanen analysed the behaviour of bureaucracies in terms of the budget-maximising bureaucrat, who is in a bilateral monopoly position with the legislature.

This approach to bureaucratic behaviour can be used to rationalise the legislative tactic of earmarking revenues for specific end-uses. There are numerous expenditures that are clearly in the public interest, but which bureaucracies may have little interest in pursuing adequately. A good example is expenditure on operations and maintenance of public structures and capital. The prestige-maximising bureaucrat generally prefers to see his department's allocation go to new and high-profile investment and construction projects rather than to something as mundane as maintaining an old road or irrigation ditch. While it is true that bureaucratic reputation may depreciate along with public structures, the process is long and managers are rarely stationary targets. As proper maintenance of the capital stock is in many countries an urgent issue, the legislature (or the executive branch) may force the bureaucracy's hand on the matter by earmarking funds for maintenance expenditures.

5. Earmarking and Intertemporal Horse-trading

Earmarking revenues can also serve to enforce long-term deals between legislators, and in the process be welfare-enhancing. Consider the case of the US Hazardous Substance Response Fund (or 'Superfund'), which obtains revenue from excise taxes on petroleum and chemicals and uses the proceeds to help clean up environmental damage caused by their production and disposal.[1] While taxing the chemical industry as a whole can be rationalised as a crude approximation to the 'polluter-must-pay' principle, one can still question the validity of earmarking the proceeds to a special fund. Why should such revenues not be assigned to—and expenditures be met from—the general fund?

Consider the following explanation. The *ex ante* probability of

---

[1] Jankowski has suggested that the Superfund is essentially a Pigovian tax. This is not correct because the supporting taxes are not intended to influence the current flow of pollution, but rather to clean up the stock of *past* environmental damage perpetrated by unknown or insolvent parties. Moreover, a *single* instrument such as the Pigovian tax on the level of effluence would be socially inoptimal for dealing with *two* issues: the clean-up of existing toxic waste and the appropriate level of future effluence. (J. E. Jankowski, Jr., 'The Practice and Prevalence of Earmarking', *Tax Institute of America Proceedings*, Columbus, Ohio: National Tax Association, 1984.)

discovering a toxic waste dump is roughly the same across the country. However, *ex post*, a legislator from Nevada has no incentive to approve clean-up expenditures in New York (because it is a pure income transfer), unless the legislator from New York can assure reciprocal support in the event of a similar disaster in Nevada at some future date. But legislators from New York cannot bind their successors to such promises. A way out of this impasse is to earmark revenues for a special fund whose expenditures do not require legislative approval. Such a one-time agreement enforces mutual promises through time and, in this instance, permits the introduction of a welfare-enhancing public activity.

It is interesting to note that the Superfund may not be used to clean up oil spills (even in the unlikely event that the perpetrator cannot be identified). This can be explained by the fact that the *ex ante* probability of an oil spill is not uniform across states. Only coastal states are concerned, and legislators from the interior of the United States will naturally oppose a long-term commitment (through an earmarked fund) for such purposes.

The rôle of earmarking in enforcing commitments between legislators can be extended to a number of situations. Eklund, for instance, points out that in societies with unstable majority coalitions, earmarking may be the only way in which new expenditure decisions can be agreed upon.[1] In the absence of such a provision, society will tend towards the *status quo*, in the process forgoing public projects with a high return to society.[2]

While the rule-enforcing aspect of earmarking enhances welfare in these cases, the opposite may also occur in practice. Special interest groups may want to earmark specific taxes as a means of limiting their tax burden. The petroleum industry, for example, may lobby for earmarking any gasoline tax for highway maintenance, if they suspect there is limited scope for expansion of this activity. Similarly, firearms manufacturers would attempt to earmark taxes levied on their industry for a complementary activity such as maintenance of wildlife.

---

[1] P. Eklund, *op. cit.*

[2] Legislators are not the only class that may resort to earmarking in such a circumstance. Wilkie (1974) and Premchand (1983) suggest that, in a number of Latin American countries, earmarking was motivated by the executive branch of government, which wanted to bypass the problem posed by legislative logrolling and unstable coalitions. (J. W. Wilkie, 'The Budgetary Dilemma in the Economic Development of Mexico, Bolivia, and Costa Rica', in D. T. Geithman (ed.), *Fiscal Policy for Industrialization and Development in Latin America*, Gainesville: University of Florida Press, 1974; A. Premchand, *Government Budgeting and Expenditure Controls: Theory and Practice*, Washington DC: International Monetary Fund, 1983, pp. 158-60.

6. Other Arguments

One justification for earmarking taxes concerns the deleterious effects of erratic financing. Revenue flows can be very unstable over the life of large public sector projects, resulting in costly heavy machinery lying idle over extended periods for want of timely and adequate funding. Earmarking receipts from a stable revenue base is a means of protecting socially important projects from the exigencies of a budgetary crunch and can, over time, be an important cost-saving device for the public sector. In terms of Figure 1, the cost schedule MCP is lowered when steady finance is made available through earmarked taxes. While earmarking serves as a constraint on budgetary flexibility, it is nevertheless argued that the inflexibility in the overall size of the budget is welfare-enhancing because there are offsetting savings in costs. It is precisely this sort of consideration that has prompted the World Bank to attach earmarking clauses to project finance in several developing countries.

Another justification for earmarking taxes is that in a number of developing countries, where democratic institutions are weak and mistrust of the government is high, earmarked taxation can improve tax compliance. If the public can be assured that taxes will be spent in their locality rather than, say, used to indulge a strongman's penchant for military expansion, they will be more willing to comply with existing taxes. In this case, earmarking acts as a substitute for lack of representative power in the executive and legislative branches of government.

Thirdly, earmarked taxes and user charges can play an important part in promoting economic stability. Consider, for example, the case of a developing country that must rely on export taxes. An exogenous decline in export proceeds would not only adversely affect the export sector but also entail cutbacks in development spending. If spending were not reduced accordingly, the alternatives—given monetary policies—are, of course, a deterioration in the balance of payments and inflation. To the extent that the tax bases underlying earmarked funds are more stable than trade taxes—user charges for roads and water may be expected to be so—macro-economic stability may be enhanced by using certain earmarked taxes.

Fourthly, many countries have in recent years been unable to muster the political will to make painful (but necessary) fiscal adjustments in the face of serious external shocks. In a number of cases, the brunt of fiscal adjustment has been borne entirely by capital and infrastructural expenditure with minimal reduction of current expenditures. While the distinction between current and development expenditure should not be exaggerated— underfunding of the recurrent costs of development expenditure is a long-standing problem in developing countries—there is a tendency to cut back on vital infrastructural and maintenance expenditures rather than on public sector employment and wages. An earmarking clause, designed to protect vital projects and expenditures, would strengthen the government's hand in reducing less socially productive components of public expenditure.

7. Summary

The normative case for earmarked taxes rests fundamentally on the assumption that groups and individuals in society have different preferences. Earmarking provides voters an opportunity to reveal their preferences for public goods with their tax dollars. This is similar to the mechanism in private markets where individuals reveal their preference for potatoes with outlays earmarked for the production of potatoes.[1] Earmarking may be loosely thought of as an application of the benefits principle of taxation since, as in private markets, taxes are paid according to perceived benefits. This is readily seen in cases where excludability in consumption is feasible, but it is difficult to implement when it is not.

The analogy with private markets also breaks down when we descend into the real world of majority voting in legislatures. However, we did establish the important proposition in sub-section 2 above that one cannot, in general, make a welfare comparison between earmarking and general fund financing since there are gainers and losers under both régimes; public choice theory provides only a *positive* analysis of earmarking. The possibility of perverse outcomes under general fund financing—such as a decline in the provision of a public good even when there is a unanimous increase in public preference for that good—is one argument against that system.

We also noted that earmarking may have a rôle as a rule-enforcing device where there is a conflict of interest with the bureaucracy; it may also facilitate a welfare-enhancing provision of public goods over a long period. Finally, it was noted that earmarking may improve both the composition of public expenditure and the stability of the budget deficit in developing countries.

With the exception of Lindahl's theory, most normative

---

[1] Whether or not the underlying distribution of income is 'just' is, of course, a separate issue.

arguments support earmarking for specific goods and services rather than advocate full-scale earmarking for all public expenditures. In addition, as a practical matter, it is important to examine instances of earmarking individually, since our positive analysis revealed that it may arise from a number of welfare-reducing causes such as rent-seeking or tax avoidance by special-interest groups.

THREE

The Case Against Earmarking

The case against earmarking is best summarised by Deran:[1]

o Earmarking hampers effective budgetary control.

o Earmarking leads to a misallocation of funds, giving excess revenues to some functions while others are undersupported.

o Earmarking imports inflexibility to the revenue structure, with the result that legislatures are hard put to make suitable adjustments when conditions change.

o Earmarking provisions often remain in force long after the need for which they were established has vanished.

o By removing a portion of fiscal action from periodic review and control, earmarking infringes the policy-making powers of state executives and legislatures.

Such criticisms derive from a particular outlook on public finance: that of the benevolent social planner attempting to maximise a well-defined social welfare function. However, the essence of the theoretical arguments for earmarking derives from a completely different view of society: one where voters with differing preferences attempt to arrive at a consensus (or at least a simple majority) to support alternative public expenditures. Thus any evaluation of earmarking should include a judgement about the appropriate model of social choice.

Even if one accepts the benevolent-social-planner approach, other difficulties remain. The arguments against earmarking implicitly assume that the alternative of general fund financing will eliminate the problems associated with earmarking. The last four of the five points listed above imply, for instance, that expenditures under general fund financing are indeed periodically reviewed and adjusted to ensure that no programme is under- or over-provided. The empirical basis for such an assertion is highly questionable. Most budgeting under general fund financing occurs incrementally

---

[1] E. Deran, 'Earmarking and Expenditures', *op. cit.*

rather than by a procedure that evaluates each tax and expenditure afresh from year to year. Any rejection of earmarking, therefore, should verify whether the public sector is indeed capable of delivering a superior result without earmarking.

Finally, the extent to which earmarking leads to rigidity in the budget should be ascertained. Many, like Premchand,[1] would argue that it is not earmarking *per se*, but rather its prevalence that is the key issue. Although widespread earmarking may induce rigidities in the budget, there are ways to reduce this effect. For example, adjustments can be made to the base or the tax rate of an earmarked pool of revenues. Alternatively, an activity can be jointly financed by both earmarked and general fund revenues, the latter providing the latitude necessary to make discretionary changes at the margin.

More fundamentally, one can question whether it is really worth making such a fuss about budgetary rigidity. Earmarked taxes are an application of the benefits principle of taxation and may be associated with higher revenues. As has been pointed out by Bird,[2] 'it makes little sense to criticise earmarking for budgetary rigidity, since without earmarking, there would be less of a budget to be rigid about'.

[1] A. Premchand, *op. cit.*

[2] R. M. Bird, *Intergovernmental Finance in Colombia: Final Report of the Mission on Intergovernmental Finance*, Cambridge, Mass.: Harvard University Law School, 1984, pp. 87-115.

FOUR

Earmarking in Practice: Colombia

No attempt is made here to provide an empirical overview of the extent of earmarking in the world economy or in any group or type of countries. Instead, we limit ourselves to the more modest objective of describing the experience of just one country, Colombia, chosen to illustrate both the beneficial rôle that can be played by earmarking and some of the pitfalls.

The complexities of the matter make it very difficult to judge whether a particular régime of earmarking has been a success or a failure. The strategy adopted here involves weighing the potential benefits of earmarking set out in Section 2 against the costs attributed to it by its detractors. A proper evaluation of the benefits requires that each instance of earmarking be considered, to use a sensible bureaucratic cliché, 'on a case-by-case basis'. A proper evaluation of the costs requires consideration of the effects of earmarking on budget formulation and overall fiscal policy. The latter requires some judgement of whether the *extent* of earmarking has reached the point where there is little room for manoeuvre in adjusting fiscal policies to changing circumstances.

Earmarking is extensive in Colombia.[1] A conservative estimate— which excludes a number of smaller earmarked taxes, as well as the retained profits of public enterprises—indicates that earmarked taxes accounted for about 45 per cent of total tax revenue in 1978. Table 1 provides a partial listing of major taxes and the expenditures for which they were earmarked. In fact, the practice of earmarking is a great deal more complex than the Table suggests, as there are numerous instances of convoluted two-tier and three-tier earmarking, where an agency receiving the proceeds of a tax is required to earmark a certain fraction of the receipts for another agency or enterprise.

Coffee Taxes: The largest class of earmarked taxes in Colombia is coffee taxes. A number of taxes are levied on coffee exports and a considerable percentage of the proceeds is earmarked for the

---

[1] This section draws heavily on Bird's *Intergovernmental Finance in Colombia, op. cit.*

Table 1:
Colombia: Earmarked Taxes, 1978

(in millions of pesos)

Tax	Destination	Amount
Coffee taxes		
Ad valorem export tax	National Coffee Fund, small portion further earmarked for Departmental Committees of Coffee Growers	2,176
Retention tax	National Coffee Fund	15,650
'Pasilla' tax	National Coffee Fund, small portion further earmarked for Departmental Committees of Coffee Growers	370
Payroll taxes		
Various taxes, different rates	National Insurance Fund (CAJANAL) and Communications Workers Social Security Fund (CAPRECOM)	1,749
Three taxes, total rate 13 per cent	Colombian Social Security Institute (ISS)	11,343
4 per cent tax	Compensation Funds	2,060
2 per cent tax	National Apprenticeship Service (SENA)	1,030
2 per cent tax	Colombian Family Welfare Institute (ICBF)	1,479
Taxes earmarked for health		
Beer tax	Sectional Health Services (SSS)	513
Liquor taxes	SSS	680
Gambling taxes	SSS, through welfare agencies (85 per cent to schools for the blind; 15 per cent to National Federation for the Blind)	862

National Coffee Fund. The organisations of growers comprising the Coffee Fund use these resources to finance various activities. Some of these expenditures can be justified on grounds of benefits taxation. For example, in 1978 the Coffee Fund spent 7 per cent of its earmarked receipts on direct benefits to growers by providing important agricultural inputs as well as infrastructure in the form of aqueducts, health and education in coffee-producing areas; in the same year, 60 per cent was retained by the Fund as part of its price stabilisation activities. Other expenditures have no rationale at all: the Fund spent 33 per cent of its receipts in 1978 to subsidise domestic coffee consumption, a questionable use of resources for a developing country.

Table 1 (Continued):

	(in millions of pesos)	
Tax	*Destination*	*Amount*
Other earmarked taxes		
Tobacco taxes	Sectional Sports Commissions; portion further earmarked	241
Gasoline taxes	National Road Fund, portion further earmarked for National Fund for Neighbourhood Roads; departmental roads; traffic departments	5,431
Hotel tax	Colombian Tourist Company (COLTURISMO)	178
Import tax	Export Promotion Fund (PROEXPO)	4,593
Valorisation taxes	To valorisation offices, for public works	994
Property tax surcharge	Regional Corporations	369
Earmarked transfers		
Tax allowance	Departments and national territories and Special District of Bogotá; 74 per cent dedicated to education and 26 per cent dedicated to health	9,900
Sales tax transfer	30 per cent of sales tax receipts granted to departments and municipalities; a large percentage is dedicated to education	1,551
Total Earmarked Taxes		**61,169**
Total Tax Revenue		132,269

Sources: R. M. Bird, *Intergovernmental Finance in Colombia, op. cit.*, Table 5-1; and *Colombia: Recent Economic Developments*, 1984.

Overall, given the Fund's surplus and the fact that a considerable portion of expenditure makes little developmental sense, one could argue that the earmarking of coffee taxes is somewhat excessive. Although the Government has already effectively de-earmarked some revenue by forcing the Fund to invest a part of its surplus in government securities, matters could be improved by reducing the amount earmarked for the Coffee Fund.

Payroll Taxes: A second major group of earmarked revenues is payroll taxes, which are mostly assigned to various social security institutions. The benefits rationale underlying earmarking is quite clear in these cases. Likewise, a benefits rationale partly applies to the Colombian Family Welfare Institute (ICBF). Among the activities financed by a separate 2 per cent payroll tax is the provision of child-care services for working couples. It is probable, however, that the earmarking provision was also motivated by a previous government's desire to ensure ICBF's survival in the future by endowing it with a generous and reliable source of revenue.

Earmarked revenues also accrue to a non-social security institution, without any apparent rationale. The Compensation Funds receive the proceeds of a 4 per cent payroll tax that is supposed to be earmarked towards payment of a family subsidy to the workers of participating firms. However, about half the proceeds have instead been financing the construction of luxury resorts run by the Funds. To the extent that most contributors are unable to utilise these subsidised facilities, this otherwise productive and easily administered tax has no benefits rationale.

Earmarking for Health: Although some sources of revenue, such as taxes on beer and liquor, do have tenuous links with ill-health, a good deal of financing for health (from taxes on gambling) has no benefits rationale. Because 'vice taxes' are heavily and successfully levied in many countries without resort to earmarking provisions, it is unlikely that they have increased total revenues in Colombia. Consequently, the true rôle of earmarking lies in assuring the health sector of a minimum level of resources. It is difficult to judge a situation such as this because there is no way of knowing whether the alternative would involve wasteful forms of military expenditure or more efficient development expenditure. The main challenge lies more in assessing whether the amounts of revenue earmarked for specific programmes (such as schools for the blind) are of the right order of magnitude.

Other Earmarked Taxes: Except for taxes on tobacco, which are earmarked for sports and cultural institutions, most other taxes can be rationalised on grounds of benefits with varying degrees of plausibility. The strongest case may be made for the valorisation tax levied on property values benefiting from public works. Bird notes approvingly that:

> '... it has been more successful in Colombia, particularly in some Colombian cities, than almost anywhere in the world. In the various studies that have been made of the valorisation tax, it has been suggested that a principal reason why that tax is acceptable is precisely that those who have to pay it perceive a relationship between the tax and the benefits that they expect to receive from the public works that it finances.'[1]

---

[1] *Intergovernmental Finance in Colombia, op. cit.*

The weakest case is that of an import surcharge earmarked for the export promotion council, PROEXPO.[1] The argument that exporters should be subsidised by importers, because 'exporters earn the foreign exchange that makes imports possible', is artificial. Most likely, the arrangement simply reflects the political power of exporters at the time PROEXPO was set up, and the Government's belief that an indirect tax in the form of an import surcharge would slip through the legislature much more readily than, say, higher income taxes.

Earmarked Transfers: Transfers from higher levels of government often reflect a revenue-sharing scheme between different levels of government and, as such, should not be considered a form of earmarking. However, the law in Colombia enjoins regional governments that receive such funds to devote 74 per cent of the transfer to current expenditure for primary education and 26 per cent to current health expenditure. Presumably, the intent of the provision is to insulate and increase total public expenditure on these functions. A recent empirical analysis by Slack and Bird[2] suggests that such tied transfers have, in practice, had the opposite effect: regions effectively used the transfers to replace locally financed health and education expenditure. This highlights the importance of carefully designing earmarking schemes that are intended to promote (or protect) particular expenditures. The promotion of health and education expenditure might have been better achieved by an open-ended matching grant.[3]

Conclusion on Earmarking in Colombia

What can be concluded from this brief summary of earmarking in Colombia? It would be difficult to argue that earmarking is so excessive that it imposes significant constraints on efficient budgeting and budget flexibility. In fact, Bird[4] asserts that it is the other way around, that earmarking is largely a *reflection* of poor budgeting and expenditure control practices:

'The structure and operation of the present budgetary and expenditure system in Colombia are such as to make it extremely difficult to spend

---

[1] This case is not far removed from the suggestion of the US auto industry some years ago that tariff revenues be dedicated to 'improving productivity' in the auto industry.

[2] N. E. Slack and R. M. Bird, 'Local Response to Intergovernmental Fiscal Transfers: The Case of Colombia', *Public Finance*, No. 3, 1983.

[3] A matching grant provides x pesos for each peso raised locally. An open-ended grant does not set a ceiling on the size of the transfer.

[4] 'Local Response to Intergovernmental Fiscal Transfers', *op. cit.*

resources efficiently. Indeed, the cumbersomeness and unreliability of this system are among the principal reasons for the marked growth of the decentralised sector and of earmarked revenues that have characterised the Colombian public sector in recent years ... Until such changes are made, it is simply Utopian to expect anyone to give up the hard-won defensive positions that have been erected in such forms as earmarked revenues and autonomous organisations, in large part as bulwarks against the perceived inefficiency of the present expenditure system.'

Although earmarking in Colombia may be viewed partly as a flight from inefficiency, this is not to suggest that the system of earmarking does not need substantial reform. It was noted that some earmarked revenues were excessive, as in the case of earmarked coffee taxes that subsidise domestic coffee consumption. In such instances, a larger fraction could be retained in the general fund. Another example involves the earmarking of 10 per cent of expenditures for the judiciary. More generally, there is clearly a need to review periodically all earmarking provisions and to verify whether funding for each activity adequately reflects changing circumstances and priorities.

FIVE

Conclusion

Having examined the case for earmarking, as well as some of the difficulties associated with its implementation, we conclude with some thoughts on the circumstances under which earmarking can be recommended.

Since the primary function of earmarking lies in facilitating the expression and resolution of differing preferences, earmarking has its greatest potential in pluralistic societies with strong democratic institutions. However, even in democracies with a broad consensus on most issues, the legislature may need to guard itself from encroachment by the military; an earmarking device that protects important social and economic expenditures can play a useful rôle in this respect.

It often happens that the only way a legislature can agree upon supporting a vital social activity is by decentralising it and removing it from routine legislative consideration. A good example of this is the US Superfund. Earmarking should be permitted when the alternative would be to forgo an activity that may broadly be deemed in the national interest.

The usefulness of earmarking is not limited to societies with active legislatures. It was noted earlier that earmarking rules may be required to force a bureaucracy into activities that it has few incentives to pursue, such as expenditure on operations and maintenance. More fundamentally, an earmarked tax can also be recommended when it is a benefits tax or a substitute for a user charge. Benefits taxation is not only appealing in terms of equity but is likely to meet with greater public compliance. This argument would apply to many activities where the beneficiaries are readily identified, for example, local services such as fire protection or small public works projects. Earmarking for such purposes does not preclude supplementary financing from general revenues, in so far as the government may also have redistributive motives. In fact, supplementary financing from general funds allows policy-makers to make discretionary changes at the margin, thus reducing the rigidities associated with earmarking.

The circumstances sketched above are far from exhaustive but do convey the general flavour of the case for earmarking. Earmarking provisions may become obsolete and counter-productive as times change; hence they should be mandatorily reviewed at regular intervals of, say, about five years. Also, the extent of earmarking should be limited to allow governments some latitude in adjusting to various shocks and exigencies as they arise.

Welfare Inefficiency of General Fund Financing

This Appendix presents a welfare-theoretical case for earmarked taxation, based on the Pareto criterion of welfare economics—that is, a situation is Pareto-efficient (or Pareto-optimal) if, and only if, no re-arrangement is possible without inflicting a loss on one or more of the participants. The main point is that the alternative to earmarked taxes, namely general fund financing, will result in non-Pareto-efficient outcomes.

Following Johansen's exposition,[1] consider an economy with a composite private good X and two pure public goods, defence (G for guns) and public order (S for security). The economy consists of two individuals (or equal groups of identical individuals), A and B. Let h denote A's 'tax share' in the financing of total expenditures ($G + S$), so that B's share is $(1 - h)$. Under general fund financing, both public goods are financed by the revenues derived from these lump-sum taxes. Each agent maximises utility subject to the corresponding budget constraint in the following two equations:

(1) A's income is the sum of A's consumption of X plus $h\,(G + S)$ or A's financing of pure public goods;

(2) B's income is the sum of B's consumption of X plus $(1 - h)$ $(G + S)$ or B's financing of pure public goods.

The assumption that each agent maximises utility subject to these constraints yields the following four further equations:

(3) A obtains the same marginal utility from an additional pound of spending on G as from an additional pound of spending on S;

(4) the marginal utility obtained by A from an additional pound of public spending on S (or G) is h times (that is,

[1] L. Johansen, 'Some Notes on the Lindahl Theory of Determination of Public Expenditures', *International Economic Review*, September 1963.

less than) the marginal utility he obtains from an additional pound of spending on X;

(5) as in (3) above for A, B obtains the same marginal utility from an additional pound of spending on G as from an additional pound of spending on S;

(6) which is the counterpart of (4) for A, the marginal utility obtained by B from an additional pound of public spending on S (or G) is $(1 - h)$ times (that is, less than) the marginal utility he obtains from an additional pound of spending on X.

For this set of six equations there are only five unknowns: G, S, h and the consumption of X by A and B. The system of equations is therefore overdetermined: in other words, no tax share h is capable of meeting all the requirements for efficiency.

One way to arrive at a determinate solution is to assume that A and B derive the same marginal utility from a pound of additional spending on G or S. Then equations (3) and (5) are duplicated, so that we are left with five equations in five unknowns. But this trivialises the whole problem of distinct and conflicting preferences.

Suppose instead that expenditures on G and S are met from two separate earmarked funds. Thus, expenditure on G is met by payment of gG by A and $(1 - g)G$ by B; likewise, for S, A pays sS while B pays $(1 - s)S$. The new budget constraints corresponding to (1) and (2) are:

(1′) A's income is the sum of A's consumption of X plus g times the supply of G and s times the supply of S;

(2′) B's income is the sum of B's consumption of X plus $(1 - g)$ times the supply of G and $(1 - s)$ times the supply of S.

The equations corresponding to (3) – (6) above are now as follows:

(3′) The marginal utility A obtains from an additional pound of public spending on G is g times (that is, less than) the marginal utility he obtains from an additional pound of his own spending on X;

(4′) Similarly, A's marginal utility from S is s times his marginal utility from X;

(5′) Similarly, B's marginal utility from G is $(1 - g)$ times B's marginal utility from X;

(6′) Similarly, B's marginal utility from S is $(1 - s)$ times his marginal utility from X.

The system now consists of six equations and six variables, and can be solved for their optimal values. The earmarking solution is necessary for Pareto-efficiency: both individuals can be made better off by moving from general fund financing to earmarking.

PART TWO

Earmarking in Britain: Theory and Practice

BARRY BRACEWELL-MILNES

The Author

DR BARRY BRACEWELL-MILNES was educated at Uppingham School, at New College, Oxford, where he read Classical Moderations and then changed to Economics, and at King's College, Cambridge, where he took his doctorate.

Dr Bracewell-Milnes now works as a consultant to academic and industrial bodies on government and international fiscal and economic policy. He was Economic Director of the Confederation of British Industry, 1968-73. Since leaving the CBI he has been Economic Adviser to The Institute of Directors, and his other appointments during the period have included Economic Consultant to the Fiscal-Economic Institute, Erasmus University, Rotterdam. In 1989 he was appointed to a Senior Research Fellowship at the IEA. He is a member of the Association of Learned and Professional Society Publishers.

He is the author of over a dozen books on taxation and other economic subjects, including *The Measurement of Fiscal Policy: An Analysis of Tax Systems in Terms of the Political Distinction between 'Right' and 'Left'* (1971); *Is Capital Taxation Fair? The Tradition and the Truth* (1974); and *The Taxation of Industry: Fiscal Barriers to the Creation of Wealth* (1981). His books on tax avoidance and evasion include *Tax Avoidance and Evasion: The Individual and Society* (1979).

For the IEA Dr Bracewell-Milnes has written 'The Economics of Tax Reduction', in *Taxation: A Radical Approach* (IEA Readings No. 4, 1970); 'Market Control over Land-Use "Planning"', in *Government and the Land* (IEA Readings No. 13, 1974); 'The Fisc and the Fugitive', in *The State of Taxation* (IEA Readings No. 16, 1977); an Epilogue, 'Is Tax Avoidance/Evasion a Burden on Other Taxpayers?', in *Tax Avoision* (IEA Readings No. 22, 1979); *Land and Heritage: The Public Interest in Personal Ownership* (Hobart Paper 93, 1982); *The Wealth of Giving* (Research Monograph 43, 1989); *Capital Gains Tax: Reform Through Abolition* (IEA Inquiry, No. 12, 1989); and 'Introduction: Tax Neutrality and Tax Policy', in *Which Road to Fiscal Neutrality?* (IEA Readings No. 32, 1990).

ONE

Introduction

This paper[1] complements the paper by Ranjit Teja both
conceptually and empirically. At the theoretical level, Teja argues
that earmarking can create wealth by improving the allocation of
resources; I argue that wealth creation is also possible through the
application of the voluntary principle to the raising of funds for
government spending. Empirically, Teja is concerned primarily with
America, I with Britain.

Earmarking, or 'hypothecation', is the designation or allocation of
particular tax revenues to particular forms of government spending.
In the strong or substantive sense of earmarking, the amount of
money available, for example, for road construction is influenced or
even strictly determined by the amount of revenue from, say, the
car duty or the excise duty on petrol (which thus acts, or can act, as
a price). The weak or nominal sense of earmarking is exemplified by
the health component of the National Insurance stamp, which has
never influenced the amount spent on the National Health Service.
There are a number of intermediate possibilities. Unless otherwise
explained, earmarking is generally used here in the strong or
substantive sense in which the amount of revenue from a particular
tax influences or determines the amount of spending for a
particular purpose. In federal states, tax revenues raised at one level
of government are often earmarked (in the strong sense) for use at
another level; and a result analogous to earmarking is produced if
revenues raised in a given district are allocated for expenditure
within that district.

Earmarking has been a neglected subject in Britain. Governments have generally preferred to do without it, because it has been
perceived as a constraint on their freedom of action; and there has
been little pressure from outside for its introduction. The present
paper argues that this neglect has been a mistake. British fiscal

---

[1] I should like to express my thanks to Arthur Seldon, joint Founder President of the
IEA, for detailed and valuable comments on a draft of this paper. Dr Bill Robinson,
Director of the Institute for Fiscal Studies, has also kindly commented on a draft. My
thanks are also due to Robert Culpin, Head of the Fiscal Policy Group, HM Treasury,
for pointing out a number of the sources in the literature of public finance.

policy has not been such a consistent success in recent years, or commanded such widespread assent, that alternatives can be prudently ignored. Other alternatives to traditional government funding through taxation include user charges, State lotteries, compulsory loans, and the sale of licences such as planning permission.[1] The purpose would always be to create wealth through an improvement of resource allocation or the extension of the voluntary principle or both.

Price Signals and the Voluntary Principle

The theory of public finance distinguishes public goods (and services) from private goods. Public goods are those which cannot be appropriated to private enjoyment; otherwise expressed, the enjoyment of a public good by one citizen does not diminish the amount available for enjoyment by others: these two definitions usually amount to the same thing—but not always.[2] By contrast, private goods are appropriated to personal use. There is also a mixed or intermediate category. Government spending funds the provision of both public and private goods: defence and street lighting are examples of the former, education and medical services of the latter. Earmarked taxes can fund the provision by government of both public and private goods; the collective provision of private goods may be susceptible of privatisation, and earmarking may assist this process, since earmarking may give a tax the quality of a price or charge: a tax is a deduction from income whereas a price or charge is an allocation of income.

The present situation is unsatisfactory because the form of collective provision adopted in Britain has suppressed price signals in more than a third of the Gross Domestic Product, even though the majority of the goods and services provided collectively are private goods, not public goods. The provision of goods 'free' at the point of consumption increases demand (in principle without limit). Monopoly provision by the State reduces or removes the pressure which competition exerts on producers to satisfy consumers. The easiest route to prosperity for these producers is to secure an increase in government spending; this is a genuine interest for

---

[1] This idea was advocated in F. G. Pennance, *Housing, Town Planning and the Land Commission*, Hobart Paper 40, IEA, 1967.

[2] In my *The Wealth of Giving: Every One in His Inheritance*, Research Monograph 43, IEA, 1989, I argue that the additional wealth created by personal giving, although fully appropriated to personal use, is a public good in the sense of a good or service, the use or enjoyment of which by one person does not reduce the amount available for use or enjoyment by others (p. 61).

government-sector producers. They are often supported in their pressure for increased government spending by elements of consumer opinion which are either under the illusion that goods provided 'free' at the point of consumption impose no costs elsewhere or else have in any case no means of assessing the marginal cost imposed on themselves (as they can very accurately in everyday purchases). Decisions are both centralised and politicised. This is the road to economic inefficiency (as recent events in Eastern Europe illustrate), since the quality of information at the centre cannot match its quality at the level of the individual consumer and since the motives of the economic agents are in any case distorted by the system. It is also the road to overprovision, although this overprovision is masked by inefficiency and underperformance.

These familiar criticisms of collective provision are complemented in the present paper by a comparison of the welfare cost to consumers of different forms of outgoing payment. In addition to the financial dimension, there is a welfare dimension, whose substance (satisfaction, utility) is the same as that of consumers' and producers' surplus or 'rent'. Some forms of payment are made more willingly than others; taxes are generally paid less willingly than other forms of payment, since the taxpayer receives nothing identifiable in return.

Earmarking or Charging?

This paper discusses earmarking in the more general context of alternatives to the funding of collective provision from a pool of undifferentiated tax revenue. Charging is the most important of a family of alternatives, each of which has advantages over funding from a tax revenue pool. The purpose is to increase the power of the taxpayer or consumer over the money he pays; this increased power leads ultimately to the right to opt out and pay for services privately, whether through insurance or directly.

There is a risk that some forms of alternative funding could be used as additional rather than alternative sources of finance, all the existing provision from tax revenue remaining in place. This would be contrary to our intention of replacing an increasing element of existing provision with superior alternatives. It is an advantage of earmarking, by comparison with other alternatives to the present system, that this risk is minimised, and the paper therefore focusses on the tighter definition of taxes through earmarking and the opportunity so offered for devolving economic power to the level of the taxpayer.

TWO

Earmarking in the Traditional Theory of Public Finance

Earmarking has generally had a poor press in the literature of public finance, at least until the last decade or two. A number of authors mention the arguments against it but none in its favour. The arguments against may be summarised as follows:

(1) Earmarking hampers effective budgetary control.

(2) Earmarking misallocates funds: excess revenues accumulate under certain headings and deficiencies under others.

(3) Earmarking imparts inflexibility to the revenue structure: the income elasticity of demand for the service and that of the earmarked tax may differ widely.

(4) Earmarking provisions often remain in force long after the need for which they were established has vanished.

(5) Earmarking infringes on the policy-making powers of governments and legislatures.[1]

Richard Goode regards earmarking as one of a number of 'violations' of 'the principle of budgetary comprehensiveness':

'Earmarking is prompted by a desire to protect particular programs, agencies, or regions from competition and to provide them larger or more stable shares of resources than they would otherwise obtain . . .'

'The prevalence of earmarking indicates a lack of confidence in the governmental system and the budgetary process.'[2]

But this assessment is in the eye of the beholder. If earmarking recognises weaknesses (or excesses) in the governmental system and the budgetary process which traditional methods of taxation ignore, then this is a merit of earmarking and not a demerit. The more serious the defects in the traditional budgetary process, the

---

[1] This summary is based on Elizabeth Deran, 'Earmarking and Expenditures: A Survey and a New Test', *National Tax Journal*, December 1965, p. 357.

[2] *Government Finance in Developing Countries*, Washington DC: Brookings Institution, 1984, pp. 12-13.

weaker the five foregoing arguments against earmarking; indeed, they may become arguments in its favour. Similarly, Goode says that 'the individualistic model ... is not a useful description of actual behaviour in democratic political systems'. But this is precisely why it is invalid to assume that democratic budgetary processes reflect voters' preferences: if voters' preferences are to be realised, or even targeted, traditional budgetary processes must be supplemented or partially replaced by surrogates of the market.

Critiques of the Traditional Theory

Even among writers on public finance there has for many· years been a strand of thought in favour of earmarking. As early as 1922, Dalton noted the arguments in favour of earmarking taxes on road users for road construction and maintenance.[1] The Musgraves note the similarity of such earmarked taxes to consumer charges, which may be both efficient and equitable. 'Second,' they say,

'linkage of voting on particular taxes with specified expenditure votes may be helpful in inducing preference revelation and thus contribute to better expenditure decisions.'[2]

The arguments in favour of earmarking are summarised by Deran:[3]

(1) Earmarking applies the benefit theory of taxation.

(2) Earmarking assures a minimum level of expenditure for desirable government functions.

(3) Earmarking can reduce the cost of specific projects by assuring continuity.

(4) Earmarking can help overcome resistance to new taxes or increased rates of tax.

Whether (3) and (4) are advantages is open to question. The obverse of (3) is that earmarking may encourage overexpenditure. As concerns (4), one libertarian doctrine of taxation is that the best form of tax is one that causes a popular uprising, like the English poll tax in 1381 or the American tea duty in 1773 or the Californian real estate tax in 1978. Similarly, it is a duty of citizenship to know something about the tax system; and this is made more difficult if the tax system is made as painless as possible. However, the insights in this argument are best answered by reducing the level of

---

[1] Hugh Dalton, *Public Finance*, London: Routledge, ninth edition, 1936, p. 182.

[2] Richard A. and Peggy B. Musgrave, *Public Finance in Theory and Practice*, New York: McGraw Hill, third edition, 1980, p. 242.

[3] 'Earmarking and Expenditures', *op. cit.*

taxation and government as a whole.[1] The theme of the present paper is wealth creation through the improvement of resource allocation and the reduction of fiscal pain; the lower the level of taxation, the stronger the case for making the reduction of fiscal pain an aim of policy rather than aiming to increase fiscal pain through improved visibility and increased taxpayer involvement.

Household and Government: Efficiency of Earmarking

On the subject of resource allocation, as Teja points out, the household analogy suggests at first sight that earmarking is restrictive and inefficient. But, even apart from the fact that household spending is voluntary and spending through the tax system coerced, there are a number of reasons why earmarking at the level of the household may be rational and efficient.

The traditional framework of public finance is neo-classical in concept, assuming perfect knowledge of benefits and instantaneous marginal adjustment of expenditure. Much more appropriate to the finances of the household (as to the finances of the State) is an Austrian conceptual framework, in which knowledge is imperfect and learning never ends; in which the process of adjustment is lengthy; and in which changes are often not small and continuous, but discrete and lumpy. Many changes in expenditure are lumpy (like an additional child or moving house), as are many income changes (like retirement or an additional job). Moreover, households (like governments) are often poor managers of money and make desirable economies and other changes, not as a result of regular and thorough reviews of the situation, but in response to external shocks so powerful that they cannot be ignored. In these circumstances, the artificial rigidities of earmarking may increase the amount of saving and improve the quality of financial management.

Eklund has argued that total government expenditure

'rarely, if ever, is subject to review. Incremental calculations proceed from existing levels of expenditure ... It is possible to infer that it is the earmarking of incremental funds, not diffusely directed to roads in general, but for specific categories of expenditure, such as for maintenance or to a region, that is crucial in determining total road expenditure.'[2]

The importance of earmarking is much increased if budgetary spending decisions are largely confined to increments and the

---

[1] The advantages of the informal economy as a means of reducing the level of taxation and government are discussed in a Peruvian context by Hernando de Soto, *The Other Path: The Invisible Revolution in the Third World*, London: I. B. Tauris, 1989.

[2] Per Eklund, 'A Theory of Earmarking Appraised', *National Tax Journal*, June 1972.

pattern of incremental spending can be influenced or even determined by earmarking.

Resource Allocation and the Voluntary Principle

The economics of public choice has made two principal contributions to the discussion of earmarking. The first is the rejection of the idea that market imperfections require correction by a government assumed to be free of these imperfections. Niskanen and others have argued that governments have their own characteristic imperfections;[1] indeed, the thrust of the public choice argument has been that the imperfections of government are more serious and less easily corrected than those of the market.[2] The second element of the public choice critique is that the self-seeking of politicians and bureaucrats and the imprecision of democratic elections as a means of taking detailed economic decisions often make earmarking a more, not less, efficient method of resource allocation than general fund financing, not least because general fund financing often produces unpredictable and paradoxical outcomes. Complementary and additional to these public choice arguments for earmarking is the argument from wealth creation through the voluntary principle, which forms the subject of the following section.

---

[1] William A. Niskanen, Jr., *Bureaucracy and Representative Government*, Chicago and New York: Aldine Atherton, 1971; *Bureaucracy: Servant or Master? Lessons from America*, Hobart Paperback No. 5, IEA, 1973.

[2] Arthur Seldon, *Corrigible Capitalism, Incorrigible Socialism*, IEA Occasional Paper 57, IEA, 1980. The authors cited in Teja's paper under 'The public choice perspective' (above, page 15) are also relevant here, particularly Buchanan and Browning.

FOUR

Wealth Creation Through the Voluntary Principle

The public choice theory of earmarking is concerned primarily with resource allocation: in the Appendix to Teja's paper, for example, the situation is Pareto-efficient[1] because each taxpayer's marginal utility from each form of government spending is equal to the relevant rate of earmarked tax. If this is not so, there is scope for increasing wealth by improving resource allocation through a move to this Pareto optimum.

This public choice analysis implicitly assumes that the cost of a tax to the taxpayer is its monetary cost; administrative and compliance costs could be incorporated in the argument at the price of additional complexity. But taxes are not all equally painful per unit of revenue raised, as is recognised by the old adage that the cost of taxation is to shear the sheep with a minimum of squealing.[2] All taxation is compulsory; but some taxes are paid more willingly than others. This relative willingness or lack of reluctance has one or other of two components: the first is the taxpayer's ignorance of what is going on and the second is his agreement (or lack of strong disagreement) with the levying of a particular tax at a particular rate. It is the second of these two elements, the approximation of taxes to compatibility with the taxpayer's voluntary behaviour, with which we are concerned here.

This process of wealth creation through the voluntary principle is not to be confused with the voluntary theory of public finance, going back to Wicksell and Lindahl, in which the voter is regarded as voting for marginal quantities of public goods whose price to him is the marginal tax he pays. And 'taxpayer's surplus', which in some treatments of the subject is a prize to be captured and spent on

---

[1] A situation is Pareto-efficient if no-one can gain without someone else losing.

[2] The original version may go back to Colbert (Controller-General of Finances under Louis XIV), who is credited with the saying that the art of taxation consists in so plucking the goose as to obtain the largest possible amount of feathers with the smallest possible amount of hissing.

something else, is here a form of wealth which public policy should seek to maximise.[1]

The creation of wealth through voluntary giving is the subject of my earlier *Research Monograph* (No. 43), *The Wealth of Giving: Every One in His Inheritance*,[2] which argues that giving, both charitable and otherwise, is a process of wealth creation and not merely of redistribution. The present argument is an extension of that of the *Monograph*. Although wealth is created by voluntary giving and destroyed by taxation,[3] wealth may be created by moving from a more to a less destructive tax system, so that certain forms of tax are in this relative sense wealth-creating.[4]

Wealth Creation and Taxpayers' Attitudes to Paying Tax

Figure 1 depicts the attitude of the taxpayer towards the payment of his taxes.[5] The vertical axis represents the taxpayer's spending, income or capital before tax and the horizontal axis represents the amount of tax revenue. The taxpayer is assumed to start with funds of OA; the line AB, with a negative slope of 45°, represents a tax or financial transfer of AC or CI through the tax system from the taxpayer to the tax authorities. Administrative and compliance costs are ignored, so that the financial loss to the taxpayer equals the financial gain to the tax revenue; in practice, administrative and

---

[1] Consumer's surplus is the excess of the utility or benefit obtained over the price paid. By analogy, taxpayer's surplus is the shortfall of the disutility of the tax below the tax paid (or the excess of the tax over the disutility). Since tax is a compulsory payment, there is a negative counterpart of taxpayer's surplus when his disutility exceeds the amount of tax paid; no analogue of this 'taxpayer's deficit' is possible in consumer spending, since a purchase will not be made if consumer's surplus is less than zero. The concepts of taxpayer's willingness and reluctance to pay taxes are discussed in my *Tax Avoidance and Evasion: the Individual and Society*, Upminster: Panopticum Press, 1979, especially pp. 82-4.

[2] *Op.cit.*

[3] Through administrative and compliance costs and excess burden.

[4] The present paper is meant to be intelligible independently of the earlier *Monograph*. However, the passages in the *Monograph* most closely related to the argument of this paper can be found in pp. 67-72 (envy and altruism), and page 83 (social loss and excess burden).

[5] The economic value of any good, service or transaction is determined on the principle of an auction, by the bid of the highest bidder. This has been mainstream economic doctrine since the development of marginal utility theory by Jevons, Menger and Walras some 120 years ago. The same principle applies when a single economic agent is deciding between different uses of his funds. The value of any good, service or transaction is subjective—its value or 'utility' to the economic agent concerned. A tax normally yields negative utility or 'disutility' to the taxpayer; this 'disutility' is less (a smaller negative) in so far as the tax is more acceptable (for whatever reason) or less unacceptable.

Figure 1:
Envy and Altruism in the Payment of Taxes

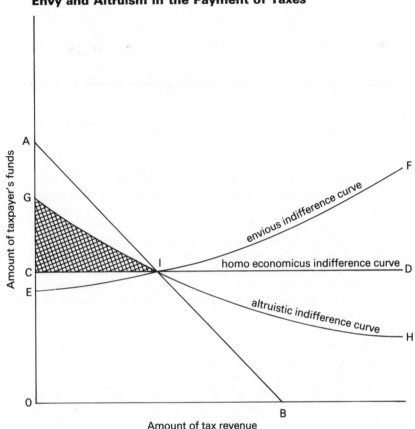

compliance costs are substantial, so that the transfer line through I is significantly steeper than AIB.[1]

An *indifference curve* shows a set of positions at which the taxpayer has the same amount of utility (or disutility); he is equally well off (or badly off) at all points on the curve. If the taxpayer is *homo economicus* and has neither envious nor altruistic feelings towards the tax authorities, his indifference curves are horizontal lines such as CD. If his feelings towards the tax authorities are

---

[1] An international comparison of administrative and compliance costs is the subject of Cedric Sandford, 'Administrative and Compliance Costs of Taxation', Deventer: Kluwer for the International Fiscal Association, Rotterdam, *Cahiers de Droit Fiscal International*, Vol. LXXIVb, 1989.

envious, he would accept a financial loss to himself as the price of securing a financial loss to the tax authorities; his indifference curve slopes upwards to the right, like EF, and may be assumed to have a positive slope that increases as his tax payments decrease.[1] If his feelings towards the tax authorities are altruistic, he would accept a financial loss to himself as the price of securing a financial gain to the tax authorities; his indifference curve slopes downwards to the right, like GH, and may be assumed to have a negative slope that diminishes as his tax payments increase.[2]

Similar phenomena can be found in commercial transactions. If a buyer considers that the seller has tried to swindle him, he may keep quiet about a subsequent mistake in his favour; he may be happy to draw the mistake to the seller's attention if he considers that the seller has given him good value or good service.

The amount of tax paid is AC or CI so that all the indifference curves pass through I. If the transfer were a voluntary payment to a charity or an individual, then (for reasons explained in Research Monograph 43) the indifference curve through A would initially be steeper than AIB and would be parallel to AIB at I. This 'donor's surplus' is not characteristic of tax payments (except occasionally in time of war or emergency); in normal times, the line AIB represents the extreme position (steepest negative slope) of the indifference curve. Along the line AI, the taxpayer is as happy to make the tax payments as to keep the money himself. By comparison with *homo economicus* he is AC better off; this is a gain to the taxpayer but not a loss to the fisc, and it is represented by the area of the triangle ACI. The shaded area GCI represents the gain of a taxpayer who is altruistic towards the tax authorities but not indifferent between their interests and his own. The gain of *homo economicus* is by definition zero; his financial loss equals his tax loss. The envious taxpayer suffers not only his financial loss but an additional loss equal to the area CIE.

Wealth can thus be created if the taxpayer's indifference curve can be moved clockwise from EIF through CID to GIH or even further. This result may be achieved by changes in the tax system that have nothing to do with earmarking, for example, a change from a tax on capital to a tax on income or a change from a tax on income to a tax on spending. But our present topic is the scope for

---

[1] This is because, as he becomes poorer (moving left along the curve), he is likely to be more concerned with survival and less with the 'luxury' of envious feelings towards the tax authorities.

[2] This is because his altruistic feelings are likely to weaken as the tax authorities become richer by reason of his tax payments and he becomes poorer.

the creation of wealth through the use of the voluntary principle, in so far as this is possible in taxation, by making taxes less like compulsory payments and more like voluntary ones (in particular, through a shift from pure taxes to parafiscal or other charges that act as prices or substitutes for prices). People make voluntary payments every day in order to obtain goods and services through the market; they may grumble about high prices, but they accept them (since otherwise the purchases would not be made).

User Charges or Benefit Taxes

As a logical extreme, taxes may be replaced by user charges as such, for example, increased charges for medical prescriptions or dental services to help fund the National Health Service. The argument for user charges based on wealth creation through the voluntary principle thus complements the argument in Arthur Seldon's book *Charge*,[1] based on improved resource allocation. And the arguments from the voluntary principle and resource allocation are still valid (although they apply less forcibly than to user charges proper) for taxes that imitate user charges or levy in some marginal relationship with benefits received.

By comparison with taxes charged on a broad base and paid into an undifferentiated Treasury fund, user charges or benefit taxes reduce demand (because taxpayers are partially deterred by the increase in price or quasi-price) and increase supply (because the process of earmarking reduces the constraints on spending for the purpose in question). Earmarking can thus have a double effect in improving resource allocation. In addition, the reduction in general taxation may increase wealth and improve resource allocation through supply-side effects (partly because taxes would then be seen in some measure as voluntary charges).

Wealth creation through the voluntary principle is thus compatible with better resource allocation; but the latter is not a necessary consequence, since demand and/or supply may be completely inelastic in response to the change of system. Similarly, better resource allocation is compatible with wealth creation through the voluntary principle; but the latter is not a necessary consequence, since there may be little or no clockwise movement of the indifference curves in Figure 1.

The practical importance of earmarking may vary from zero to

---

[1] London: Temple Smith, 1977. The argument is taken further in the same author's *Capitalism*, Oxford: Blackwell, 1990, although the subject matter of the latter book is much wider.

100 per cent: the absolute amount of a particular type of government spending, or the increase in that level,[1] may be unaffected or wholly determined by the amount of earmarked taxation. Even if the level of government spending is unaffected, however, and the earmarking is purely formal, it may nevertheless serve the useful purpose of increasing public awareness of the cost of government spending in different forms.

---

[1] See above, page 49.

FIVE

Earmarking in British Fiscal Practice

The best known and most important examples of earmarking in 20th-century British fiscal practice are the 1920s Road Fund and a number of funds under the heading of social security provision. This section first describes these two major categories of fund and then discusses other types of charge that are formally or substantially related to particular forms of expenditure. It concludes with a brief note on the earmarking of expenditure.

The Road Fund

The Road Fund was established under sections 2 and 3 of the Roads Act 1920. On the date of its establishment, 1 January 1921, there were transferred to the Road Fund all monies and investments standing to the account of the Road Improvement Fund set up under the Development and Road Improvement Funds Act 1909.

The principal receipts of the Road Improvement Fund during the years 1911 to 1916 inclusive were motor spirit duties and carriage licences.[1] By the Finance Act 1915, the share of the proceeds of the carriage duties and the whole of the net proceeds of the motor spirit duty, which were previously paid into the Road Improvement Fund, were retained in the Exchequer as from August 1915. From 1 April 1920, these sources of revenue were again credited to the Road Improvement Fund; but they again ceased with the introduction of the new system in 1921. Thereafter the Road Fund's tax revenue came from the licence duties on mechanically propelled vehicles imposed from January 1921 (also variously described in the Road Fund's accounts as Motor Tax Account, Motor Taxation Receipts and Issues from the Consolidated Fund). Receipts from this source were £10·8 million in 1922 and £27·4 million in 1936-37. Small supplementary sources of income were added under the Road Traffic Act 1930 (fees for drivers' licences), the Road and Rail Traffic Act 1933 (fees for goods vehicle licences), and the Road Traffic Act 1934 (fees for driving tests). The income of the Fund was originally supplemented by an Exchequer

---

[1] *Road Fund Report 1921-22*, Appendix 14.

grant; but the last such grant was made in 1923, and within a few years the Fund was making repayments to the Treasury.

The principal substantive outgoings from the Road Improvement Fund and the Road Fund were grants to local authorities for road construction and maintenance. However, the amount available for this purpose was much reduced by annual payments towards the General Exchequer contribution under the Local Government Acts 1929 and single payments under section 32 of the Finance Act 1935 and section 33(3) of the Finance Act 1936. These payments amounted to over 40 per cent of all disbursements in 1936-37.

The principal change came under the Finance Act 1936 and the Trunk Roads Act 1936. Motor taxation receipts (motor vehicle licence duties) were discontinued from April 1937 and re-placed by the Parliamentary Grant in Aid. The Road Fund itself was abolished under section 4 of the Miscellaneous Financial Provisions Act 1955.

Government raids on the Road Fund

Thus governments raided the Road Improvement Fund in 1915 and the Road Fund in 1929, 1935 and 1936, and ended the hypothecation of vehicle excise duties in 1937. Thereafter, the Road Fund had no income of its own and became merely an agency administering the grant in aid. The Second Report from the Select Committee on Estimates for the 1953-54 session said that

'it would lead to greater clarity in the Estimates and more information being available to Members if the Road Fund were abolished, and expenditure on roads provided for in a normal departmental Vote'.

This was the line taken by the Financial Secretary to the Treasury (Mr Henry Brooke) when moving the Miscellaneous Financial Provisions Bill.[1]

The arguments for abolishing the Road Fund in its debilitated post-1937 condition, however, are not arguments for raiding in 1915, 1929, 1935 and 1936, nor for abolishing hypothecation in 1937. All these attacks on the Road Fund were widely deplored at the time. If the institution of a Road Fund is desirable in itself, it should not be frustrated simply because the government cannot be trusted to keep its fingers out of the till: the untrustworthiness of government in this respect is an argument for more, not fewer, restrictions on government discretion and is conformable with the general thrust of public choice analysis. Changes to correct these institutional defects of the present system are proposed below

---

[1] *Hansard*, 1 July 1955 (Vol. 543), col. 665.

(page 73). It can also be argued against earmarking that the link between taxation and benefits is factitious (as in the National Insurance Fund, below): but the rejoinder is the same, namely that the link should be strengthened and made more substantial, not weakened or destroyed on the ground that it has not been working properly. The most radical way of resolving or alleviating this problem is to reduce the scope of government activity.

The Road Fund and earmarking—similar principles

The arguments of substance used in favour of the Road Fund at the time of its introduction correspond closely to the theoretical arguments in the present paper—the voluntary principle of wealth creation and the benefits principle of taxation. In moving the Second Reading of the Roads Bill, Sir Eric Geddes, the Minister of Transport, called the new system 'an extraordinary example of voluntary taxation'[1] (and thus comparable with market pricing). The Fund was to be spent on roads. The Parliamentary Secretary to the Ministry of Transport said:

'Under the Development and Roads Improvement Funds Act 1909, there are certain definite uses to which the fund must be applied. These are the improvement of existing roads and the construction of new roads. By the present Bill it is proposed to enlarge those powers to some slight extent by putting in the maintenance of roads.'[2]

Sir Eric Geddes said:

'Although those terms [the Finance Act provisions for the expenditure of the fund] have not taken the form of an enactment, nevertheless they have been treated as binding upon us in every respect as a bargain with the community.'[3]

Promises, promises. Within a few years the raids had begun. Both the raids and the subsequent abolition of hypothecation were justified on the broad grounds that the situation had changed, that Parliament was still sovereign and that Parliaments and Ministers could not bind their successors. Public choice theory has shown the weakness of these arguments as a basis for economic decisions.

The history of the Road Fund thus has lessons to teach in the use of earmarking today, both for road taxation and more generally. Ministerial promises are unreliable except in the very short term. They are not bankable. The 'binding bargain with the community' brings to mind the 'social compact' or 'social contract' from the heyday of prices-and-incomes policy; this had a short life

---

[1] *Hansard*, 2 December 1920 (Vol. 135), col. 1,491.

[2] *Ibid.*, col.1,528.   [3] *Ibid.*, col. 1,493.

expectancy (it was immediately dubbed the 'social contrick') and a short life. Even if a Minister keeps his own promises, they may be cheerfully broken by successors from the same party, let alone another party. Public choice theory has shown how under a democratic system the public interest may and often will be suppressed by the pressure of sectoral interests. Thus the Road Fund was an easy target (as for similar reasons a Budget surplus or Public Sector Debt Repayment (PSDR) is an easy target today for pressure groups seeking additional government spending). The Road Fund was first damaged and debilitated, its financial and intellectual integrity compromised and destroyed; what remained was then attacked as lacking any rational justification and unceremoniously removed. The enemies of earmarking, their motives and their arguments, are much the same now as they have been over the last 70 years. Whatever the advantages of earmarking for economic efficiency and wealth creation, it is unlikely under present institutional arrangements that earmarking will enjoy a fair wind and a calm passage.

If the advantages of earmarking are to be realised, present centralised decision-taking in response to lobbying should be shifted towards a devolved system of decision-taking in response to individual preferences. Possibilities include semi-autonomous government agencies and local government authorities. It is even possible for government provision to be privatised, with contractors competing for the use of earmarked taxes to provide a specified service. In any case, the agency should have sufficient independence of government to be able to mount an effective defence against raids.

Even nominal earmarking could help to control the growth of government spending by making it clearer that the beneficiaries of this spending and the taxpayers who pay for it are in large measure the same people. But substantive earmarking could provide a more effective control if a tranche of spending were transferred from pooled to earmarked tax revenue as its source of funding, the agency being denied access to pooled tax revenue as a source of funds for additional spending.

Possible sources of income for a resurrected Road Fund include petrol excise duty, value added tax on petrol, car tax, vehicle licences, parking fees, fees for driving tests, and any future congestion tax. Possible uses of these funds include the construction of new roads (including overheads such as public inquiries and the compensation of dispossessed landowners); the maintenance of existing roads; and the funding of driving tests. Given that new roads are now often regarded, not as public goods, but as public 'bads' by reason of the damage they do to the environment, earmarking could impart an element of objectivity into an area of decision-taking that is at present largely subjective and arbitrary.

Social Security

The coverage of British social security provision has included unemployment, industrial accidents and diseases, sickness and invalidity, disability (attendance allowance), old age, war pensions, death (death grant), bereavement (widows and orphans), family endowment (family allowances, child tax allowance, child benefit), maternity (maternity allowance), social assistance (national assistance, supplementary benefit income support), low pay (family credit), and difficulty in paying for accommodation (housing benefit).

A number of these provisions have or have had their own funds. The Appendix (below, page 101) identifies the National Health Insurance Fund, the Central Fund, the Unemployment Fund, the Pensions Account, the Treasury Pensions Account, the National Insurance Fund, the National Insurance (Reserve) Fund, the Industrial Injuries Fund, the Redundancy Fund, and the Maternity Fund. These have had their own sources of income and are thus to be distinguished from an entity such as the Social Fund which has specified obligations but is supported financially by payments out of general departmental reserves (Social Security Act 1986, section 32(6)).

The Appendix indicates that there was no long-term consistency of government policy in establishing and maintaining these various funds. It illustrates the tension between the wish to hypothecate money separately for each purpose and the temptation to use for one purpose money originally hypothecated for another. This temptation was all the stronger since the resources available in the various funds had relatively little influence on the amounts disbursed, at least in the longer term.

A key proposal of the Beveridge Report[1] was the unification of social security. As is noted in the Appendix, the National Insurance Fund was set up to amalgamate 13 previously separate funds. Thereafter the National Insurance Fund was more important than all other social security funds combined.

---

[1] *Social Insurance and Allied Services*, London: HMSO, Cmd. 6404, 1942, pp. 15, 20.

Beveridge and the contributory principle

The National Insurance Fund has always been financed on the contributory principle, at least in name. The Beveridge Report says: 'the contributory principle was emphasised or accepted by all the organisations most widely representative of insured persons in Britain' (para. 274). Beveridge discussed the contrast between individual and collective insurance (such as social insurance); but he was not prepared

> 'to abandon insurance contributions entirely in favour of taxation according to capacity. From the point of view adopted in this Report and advocated by the great majority of the organisations, and persons who gave evidence to the Committee, the suggestion involves a departure from existing practice, for which there is neither need nor justification and which conflicts with the wishes and feelings of the British democracy' (para. 273).

All British Governments since 1911 have seen a rôle for hypothecation in this area of policy, and the Thatcher Government made its position clear in the 1985 Green Paper, *Reform of Social Security*:

> 'The principle that entitlement to benefits should be related to contributions paid is an important one to which the Government is firmly committed. People do not regard their contributions as just another tax: they realise that they are earmarked to finance benefits. The Government believe that it is right to retain a link between contributions paid in and benefits received.'[1]

Despite these words, the contributory principle endorsed by Beveridge has been progressively weakened by successive governments, the Thatcher Government as much as any (not least through its abolition of the ceiling on employers' contributions in 1985, apparently in response to a short-term revenue deficiency). Even the resulting system is defensible on the ground that eligibility for contributory benefits requires a minimum level of contributions (although entitlement may not be increased by contributions above this level); but in practice the existing contributory principle is not often supported by rational explanation of any kind. This incoherence of doctrine is exemplified by an extract from the proceedings of a Parliamentary Committee.

Q (MP): 'How on earth are the contribution requirements fixed and what relationship do they bear to the marvellous benefits they unlock?'

A Expert witness (Under Secretary in the Family Support and

---

[1] *Reform of Social Security*, Cmnd. 9517, London: HMSO, 1985.

Supplementary Benefit Division of the Department of Health and Social Security): 'They are not fixed on any particularly rational basis but on the basis that you want a reasonable test and do not want to make it too hard for people to get the benefits . . . The working generation today basically pays for the pensions of the generation which has now retired and we go forward in the hope that each successive generation will, in return for something which is much less than full value, go on doing so. I do not think there is a particular sort of logic to any particular figure.'[1]

A common reaction to this doctrinal incoherence is to argue that national insurance contributions are no more and no less than a tax and that they should be so regarded and treated. The present paper, by contrast, argues that the fault lies, not in the contributory principle itself, but in the failure to articulate it properly (in particular, through privatisation). This failure in turn wastes the wealth that could be recaptured from the tax system by means of the voluntary principle; the scope for this form of wealth creation is exemplified by the provisions in the 1989 Budget offering incentives to opt out of the State Earnings-Related Pensions Scheme (SERPS), an arrangement which must have been attractive to the individuals opting out (because they were volunteers) as well as to the Government (which disburdened itself of unsustainable long-term liabilities).

The weakening of the contributory principle was not planned or desired; it was the result of demographic pressures in the 1970s. It was inherent in the 1911 unemployment and health schemes that contributions were actuarially related to benefits. There was a contribution from the Treasury from the beginning in order to increase the levels of benefit above what would have been possible otherwise and make 'social insurance' (pooling of risks) worthwhile for those who would have been better-than-average risks in private schemes. The funds were meant to balance taking one year with another, and they built up substantial surpluses over good periods.

---

[1] Extract from Minutes of Evidence, Subcommittee of the House of Commons Treasury and Civil Service Committee, Session 1982-83, paras. 838-41, cited in Dilnot, Kay and Morris, *The Reform of Social Security*, Institute for Fiscal Studies/ Oxford University Press, 1984, pp. 23-34. The unsubstantiated hope of those currently paying national insurance contributions that others will, in due time, be willing to pay for their retirement pensions and other benefits has been described as 'the contract between the generations'; see my comment on the 'social contract' or 'social compact' (above, p. 59). The fraudulent nature of any alleged 'contract between the generations' is a main theme of Arthur Seldon, *Pensions for Prosperity*, Hobart Paper 4, IEA, 1960.

Beveridge argued (paras. 241-243) that there should be a transition period of some 20 years with rising pension rates; contributory pensions should rise gradually to the full subsistence level supported by contributions, means-tested non-contributory assistance pensions being granted meanwhile to those in need. Although this advice was rejected (mainly for political reasons) and full benefit was made payable immediately to new entrants to the insurance scheme, the National Insurance Fund remained in surplus for some 10 years. In the late 1950s, the combination of a growing number of pensioners and an increasing level of general prosperity (with the implication that subsistence income for the 'needy' ought to increase correspondingly) threatened to drive the Fund into deficit: rather than make good the deficit from taxation, the Government preferred to raise current contributions from employers and employees (and did so in large measure by relating them to income—contributions were entirely income-related by 1975).

Thus a system of benefit entitlement based on contributions paid was replaced by a system of pay-as-you-go, and the notion of funding required for actuarial insurance was abandoned. The Exchequer share of the expenditure of the Fund rose during this period from 6 per cent of total expenditure in 1950 to 20 per cent in 1960. It was fixed at 18 per cent of all other contributions by the 1975 Social Security Act (section 1(5)). By the mid-1980s the Treasury's supplement to the National Insurance Fund was some 5 per cent of total social security spending, and falling; it was abolished with effect from 6 April 1989 and absorbed in the contribution from the Consolidated Fund (general taxation).

Restoring the contributory principle

The thesis of the present paper is that contributions linked actuarially to benefits are preferable to pay-as-you-go contributions (for reasons given by Beveridge[1] and others), and that the funding of social security benefits through separate National Insurance contributions (NICs) is preferable to their funding through general taxation (because funding through general taxation is least conformable to the voluntary and benefit principles). By this argument, the absorption of NICs into general taxation would yield the worst of all results, consisting of a massive and permanent increase in general taxation. This result would be particularly

---

[1] Beveridge Report (*Social Insurance and Allied Services*), *op. cit.*, especially paras. 10, 21, 24, 266, 274, 375-384; Appendix A, paras. 12-32, 91.

Table 1:
Department of Social Security Expenditure
Plans, 1990-91

	£ million
Contributory benefits	
Retirement pensions and Christmas bonus	23,110
Widows' benefits	964
Unemployment benefit	962
Invalidity benefits	4,544
Sickness benefit	223
Industrial injuries benefits	569
Maternity allowance	31
Guardian's allowance	1
Estimated outgo on National Insurance Fund benefits	**30,404**
Statutory sick pay	939
Statutory maternity pay	298
Total contributory benefit expenditure	31,641
National Insurance Fund administration	1,024
Total expenditure met from the National Insurance Fund	**32,666**
Non-contributory benefits	
Pensions	736
Disability benefits	2,881
Income support	8,461
Family benefits	5,314
Housing benefit	100
Total voted in Estimates	**17,492**
Expenditure met from the Social Fund	152
Total non-contributory benefit expenditure	17,644
Total non-contributory benefit administration	1,724
Total non-contributory benefit cost	**19,368**

[*Table 1 contd. on p. 66*]

ironical given that it was what the increase in NICs in the late 1950s and thereafter was intended to avoid; but the progressive weakening of the contributory principle for reasons of short-term expediency (political as well as financial) has strengthened the lobby for the absorption of NICs into general taxation. Since there is little or no rational justification for the present system, the logic of our argument is that the contributory principle should be restored and strengthened, through privatisation or otherwise.

Table 1 gives the detail of the Department of Social Security expenditure plans for 1990-91. Total expenditure is £55·6 billion,

Table 1 (Continued):

	£ million
Total central government's own expenditure	
Contributory benefits	32,666
Non-contributory benefits	19,368
Total central government's own expenditure	**52,034**
of which Voted in Estimates	19,216
Non-voted	32,818
Central government grants to local authorities	
Rent rebates and allowances	1,677
Community charge benefit/rebates	1,756
Housing benefit local authority administration	113
Total	**3,546**
Total Department of Social Security expenditure	
Central government's own expenditure	52,034
Central government grants to local authorities	3,546
Total	**55,580**
of which benefits	52,718
administration (£1,024m. + £1,724m. + £113m.)	2,862

Sources: *Report by the Government Actuary on the drafts of the Social Security Benefits Up-rating Order 1990 and the Social Security (Contributions) (Re-rating) Order 1990*, Cm. 948, London: HMSO, January 1990, Appendix 4. *The Government's Expenditure Plans 1990-91 to 1992-93*, Cm. 1014, London: HMSO, January 1990, Ch. 14, Table 14.

of which £52·7 billion is benefits and £2·86 billion is costs of administration. Of this £55·6 billion, £52·0 billion is central government's own expenditure and £3·5 billion central government grants to local authorities. The £52 billion of central government's own expenditure consists of £32·7 billion of contributory benefits and £19·4 billion of non-contributory benefits. The financing of the £31·6 billion of 10 items of contributory benefits (= £32·7 billion *minus* £1 billion of administrative costs) gives an idea of the potential for wealth creation through a more effective and better articulated system of hypothecating National Insurance contributions into private insurance.[1]

---

[1] One method of so doing would be to hypothecate part of National Insurance contributions and to use this money to fund a financial incentive to the citizen to bear his own risks instead of having them financially supported by the government: risks would be borne by private insurers on payment of a fee instead of by the government on the strength of the taxing power.

Table 2:
Percentage of DSS Programme Income Provided by Each Source of Finance

	1989-90 estimated outturn (percentages)
National Insurance Fund investment income	2
Treasury supplement to National Insurance Fund	0
Insured persons' national insurance contributions	25
Employers' national insurance contributions	29
Consolidated Fund (general taxation)	44
	100

Source: Cm. 1014, op. cit., Table 14.5.

Table 2 shows the situation from the income side. In 1989-90, the estimated outturn for shares of Department of Social Security income shows NICs as accounting for 54 per cent of the whole and general taxation for 44 per cent. These proportions of a total Departmental expenditure of well over £50 billion give an indication of the scope for wealth creation, first, through a better articulation of the contributory principle and, second, through the extension of earmarking to items at present funded out of general taxation.

Table 3 shows the estimated income and outgo of the National Insurance Fund in 1990-91, the same year as for Table 1. About 96 per cent of the National Insurance Fund share of National Insurance contributions comes from Class 1 contributions levied on employed earners and their employers. Contributions are net of some £7·6 billion of contracted-out contribution reductions. The balance in the Fund at the end of the year, £7,686 million, although still substantial (a quarter of turnover), has been declining rapidly.

The total outgo on benefits of £30,408 million is substantively the same figure as the £30,404 million in Table 1. Statutory sick pay (SSP) of £930 million and statutory maternity pay (SMP) of £296 million in Table 3 are recovered by employers from NICs and are excluded from both totals and also from the contributions of £27,858 million in Table 3. This expenditure is being funded from general taxation for the first time in 1990-91, because under the terms of the Social Security Bill there are no contribution conditions. By the criteria of the present paper this move from NICs to general taxation is retrograde.

Table 3:
Estimated Income and Outgo of the
National Insurance Fund, Great Britain, 1990-91

	£ million
Income	
Contributions	27,858
State scheme premiums	220
Investment income	750
Transfer from Redundancy Fund	1,000
Total	**29,828**
Outgo	
Benefits:	
At present rates	28,285
Increases due to proposed changes	2,123
Total	30,408
Transfers to Northern Ireland	180
Administration	966
Total	**31,554**
Income total	29,828
Outgo total	31,554
Excess of outgo over income	*1,726*
Balance in Fund at the end of the year	**7,686**

Source: Report by the Government Actuary on the drafts of the Social Security Benefits Up-rating Order 1990 and the Social Security (Contributions) (Re-rating) Order 1990, Cm. 948, January 1990, p. 2.

'Fiscalisation' of National Insurance premiums

The central fault of the present social security system is that it 'fiscalises' and nationalises insurance premiums running to tens of billions of pounds a year. 'Fiscalisation' is the process of turning a voluntary, commercial payment into a tax; it destroys wealth for the reasons explained in Section 4: 'Wealth creation through the voluntary principle', above. Nationalisation, in insurance as anywhere else, suppresses competition and destroys wealth by increasing inefficiency. National Insurance is also, by comparison with genuine insurance, a risky method of laying off risks: future entitlements depend, not on the contractual obligations of a financial house, but on whatever current government policy may happen to be in 10, 30 or 50 years' time. In particular, within the time-scale that is of interest to most British readers of this paper, a future government might decide to means-test entitlement to the State retirement pension with retrospective effect; this would hardly be more radical than the present Government's decision in 1985 to remove the ceiling on employers' National Insurance contributions, thus increasing contributions without increasing benefits correspondingly. It is also a serious fault of the present system that the State effectively limits spending on contributions (because different risks are not separately insured) or on benefits (such as the amount of spending on the NHS, which is centrally determined), or on both.

Most of the risks listed in Table 1 are or have been insured commercially, and almost all could be commercially insurable if the State paid part or even the whole of the premiums of the poorest minority or premiums for risks otherwise unacceptable commercially. This would be a much more economical use of public funds than the present system. Even unemployment is an actuarially insurable risk, as was established by the 1911 scheme; and at present the self-employed (many of whom have incomes well below the national average) are obliged to bear the risk of unemployment themselves, since no provision for this risk is made by the State system.

There is no good reason for the involvement of the State in any of these areas beyond the subsidisation of commercial insurance premiums for a minority of the population. On the contrary, the State and the citizen have a common interest in getting the former off the back of the latter, as was demonstrated by the unexpected success of the privatisation of SERPS (State Earnings-Related Pension Scheme). The present system was not designed by anyone but has evolved as a result of short-term responses to external shocks (like the weakening of the contributory principle in response to demographic pressures in the 1970s).

The way forward

The way forward is to move in the opposite direction to that followed by governments of both parties over the last generation. The contributory principle should be re-instated and strengthened, in particular by the restoration of the ceiling for employers' National Insurance contributions. The collective insurance of risks should be privatised like SERPS, on terms attractive both to the government and to the taxpayer (if necessary, through the use of a government subsidy). The privatisation of the State retirement pension imposes a once-and-for-all cost as the pay-as-you-go principle ceases to work effectively: a generation of pensioners whose pensions would have been funded by their successors on the pay-as-you-go principle now has to be funded otherwise, since these successors are using the money to fund their own pensions on actuarial principles. Since this is a once-and-for-all cost incurred in moving to sounder financial principles, there is a strong case for funding most or all of this cost from an increase in the national debt.

The additional cost of moving from pay-as-you-go social insurance to funded commercial insurance is most acute for retirement pensions with their extended time-scale of premiums and pension payments. For the other insurable risks, funds can be built up over a much shorter period. Contributions should be subdivided and paid into separate earmarked funds, as was the practice earlier, which could eventually be sold. The substantive hypothecation of contributions into earmarked funds would transform the elements of nominal hypothecation in the present system and restore the commercial principle that separate risks should be handled separately. The separate funds should be given strong Boards and distinct identities in order to reduce the risk of government interference and raids.

The subdivision of contributions and their hypothecation into earmarked funds also facilitates the privatisation of the various risks in the manner of SERPS, on terms attractive to both the government and the individual. Since this applies to existing entitlements and not simply to new ones, this buying out by the government of its future liabilities could hasten the process of privatisation substantially. And the independence of the various funds would be much enhanced if the individual were able to top up his contributions and thus his entitlements; a form of this system of additional voluntary contributions is to be found in the existing provision whereby a pensioner can postpone drawing his State pension in the interest of increasing his entitlements later.

Thus, most or even all the elements of National Insurance giving entitlement to contributory benefits should be privatised; and the same may be possible for certain non-contributory benefits as well. A minority of contributions could be subsidised by the government. The lesson of SERPS shows that privatisation of National Insurance can be attractive both to the government and to the individual. As an interim measure assisting the passage to eventual privatisation, National Insurance contributions should be subdivided and hypothecated into funds earmarked for the various benefits. Additional voluntary contributions should be acceptable and would strengthen the independence of the funds. Funds run more and more on commercial lines could eventually be privatised by sale; and this form of privatisation would be additional to the movement from National Insurance to commercial insurance of new risks taken on after a certain date.

Other Examples

The Road Fund and National Insurance have an important place in the history of earmarking in Britain because both have had a recognisable institutional structure that has been lacking in other examples of earmarking ranging from the formal to the substantial.

An example of purely formal earmarking was the 1937 National Defence Contribution, succinctly described in the 1982 Green Paper on Corporation Tax:

> 'In 1937 the National Defence Contribution was introduced at the rate of 5 per cent as a contribution to the national defence effort. On the outbreak of war in 1939 this was supplemented by the Excess Profits Tax. The Excess Profits Tax was repealed in 1947—partly to avoid the risk of heavy repayments of tax with the expected fall in the level of profits—and the National Defence Contribution (which itself had originally been conceived as a temporary tax) was put on a permanent basis under the name of the Profits Tax.'[1]

This was labelling for political reasons rather than earmarking in any substantive sense of the term, since military spending was unaffected and there was not even a separate fund. Here the purpose of labelling was to make heavy tax burdens more acceptable to other taxpayers. A more recent example of labelling is the proposal (not so far adopted) to divide the basic rate of income tax between a National Health Service component and the rest, in order to bring home to people how much the NHS is costing them individually.

At the other end of the scale are charges for government goods and services. These affect demand and may also affect supply if the incomes of providers are largely composed of the amounts charged. They are taxes levied on the benefit principle rather than earmarked taxes, since the volume and quality of the goods and services provided may be unaffected by the amounts charged; and they are not paid into a separate fund. Nevertheless, charges represent benefit taxation in an extreme form; and some systems of charging may exert a strong or even determining influence on the quality and quantity of the provision.

---

[1] *Corporation Tax* (consultation paper), Cmnd. 8456, London: HMSO, 1982, Appendix 1, p. 124.

Earmarking is normal for government spending in Britain, since Departmental expenditure is voted in considerable detail: £88·5 billion of supply estimates was subject to cash limits in 1990-91 and a further £14·5 billion to running costs limits, a total of £103 billion or some 58 per cent of the central government expenditure planning total. Whereas the raiding of earmarked taxes is often regarded as normal or even financially and politically respectable, earmarking of funds for particular forms of spending may be an effective constraint in practice and the subject of criticism if it is not. For example, in a report published on 12 March 1990, the Parliamentary Social Services Committee said that local authority funds to help the elderly and mentally ill live at home rather than be sent to hospital would be spent on other things unless the Government agreed to earmark funds for community care.

All these examples show how discretionary spending financed out of general taxation may be regarded as inferior to an articulated system of labels and constraints in which outcomes are at least identified or perhaps influenced or even determined in accordance with the benefits principle of taxation and the preferences of taxpayers. Section 6 discusses the range of possibilities.

SIX

Earmarking and
Other Alternative Medicines

This section discusses the range of alternatives to the orthodox fiscal medicine of paying for government spending out of pooled tax revenues. The orthodox medicine might be superior to the alternatives if Parliamentary and governmental control over government spending were effective; but these controls are ineffective, for reasons explained by the theory of public choice. As things are, alternative medicines have one or more of the advantages over orthodox medicine that they improve the allocation of resources on the demand side or the supply side or both; and/or that they make payments less unacceptable to the taxpayers and thus increase wealth through the voluntary principle; and/or that they increase the acceptability of payments in a political sense through adherence to the benefits principle of taxation. The following nine headings list the main possibilities, starting with government spending itself and moving on to payment for this spending otherwise than from pooled tax revenues.

(i) Earmarking of Spending by Government Departments

If monies unspent at the end of a financial year by a government department or other government agency must be returned to the Treasury and absorbed into the pool of general tax revenue and other government funds, there is a strong incentive to use the funds uneconomically (though within the constraints imposed by official audit), since the value of the funds to the department, even if they are spent wastefully, will generally exceed their value to the department if they are returned to the Treasury (this latter value being normally zero). This is the case for virement or viring, a provision enabling a department to carry over unexpended funds from one financial year to the next. Viring is a form of earmarking; although the subject is beyond the scope of the present paper, it illustrates the potential of earmarking for improving the control of government spending, even when the source of funds for this spending is given.[1]

(ii) Earmarking of Spending by Individual Citizens

The relief of poverty is more efficient if it takes the form of payments in unfettered cash rather than in 'free' or subsidised goods or services; and tied payments to individuals may represent an efficiency gain if what these payments replace is 'free' goods or services, perhaps with little or no element of individual choice. Markets are created by the distribution of cash and destroyed by distribution in kind.

The present Government has capitulated in the face of the vested interests that feared the competition that would be created by education vouchers; but it has brought in a system of vouchers for training. The advantages of training vouchers and education vouchers are similar. While they are inferior to some form of private funding (if that is attainable), they are superior to other forms of provision by the State.

(iii) Government Spending and Charitable Activity

The advantages of replacing government spending with charitable activity (and of using more generous tax reliefs as incentives to this end) constitute a main theme of *The Wealth of Giving*.[2] Wealth is created through the replacement of compulsory by voluntary funding; there may be efficiency gains as well; and the replacement of government monopoly by competition between charities has the political as well as economic advantages of devolution and decentralisation.

Charities often run earmarked appeals for funds: more money may be raised in this way than if all sums raised were pooled in a general fund. This holds good even though the amounts spent on the different earmarked causes may (quite properly) be unaffected by the amounts subscribed. If a charity launches an appeal for a particular cause, intending to make good any shortfall from general funds, then the cause concerned does not lose if the amount subscribed falls short of the amount of the appeal. Any surplus may be left with the cause concerned or transferred to closely related

---

[1] The development of the end-year flexibility scheme (EYF), introduced by the Treasury in 1983, is the subject of Colin Thain and Maurice Wright, 'Conceding Flexibility in Fiscal Management: the Case for Public Spending End-year Flexibility', *Fiscal Studies*, November 1990.

[2] *Op. cit.*

causes or to general funds; the second and third of these choices require prior notice if subscribers are not to feel aggrieved.

The logic of the argument is directly applicable from earmarked charitable appeals to earmarked taxes.

(iv) Lotteries

Even if lotteries were untaxed, they would be a negative-sum game as a result of administrative costs; and taxation increases the collective loss they create for the participators. Lotteries are nevertheless big business, supported by a large army of volunteers. The punters are not irrational, as some prim theorists suggest; they are merely giving Fortune a chance. Traditional welfare theory and redistributive economics teach the wrong lesson here. Welfare is not reduced by regressive redistribution. The money that is scarcely missed in small quantities from many contributors may do some real good when concentrated in a small number of large heaps.

There is a real welfare gain if taxation is replaced by the proceeds of a lottery, because volunteers replace conscripts. The argument implies that revenue from this source should be maximised, at least as long as taxation remains at anywhere near its present levels. The private interest deserving protection is not those with moral scruples about gambling (since they are not obliged to participate), but the private-sector lottery industry, which is in danger of suffering from subsidised competition. To keep the playing field level, the proportion of total stake money retained for the National Health Service in an NHS lottery, for example, should be no lower than the proportions extracted from private-sector lotteries in betting duty and corporation tax.

(v) Charging

Even if the provision of goods and services by the State or local authorities is generally inefficient, the damage done is diminished by the imposition of charges sufficient to make these activities self-supporting.

Examples at municipal level include charges for swimming baths and sports grounds. Even libraries that lend for nothing often impose fines for books overdue. At the national level, the charge that affects most households is the television licence. An industrial example is the charges for research services made to business clients by university departments, which are largely funded with government money.

The provision of driving tests is a hard-core government responsibility (even though this need not preclude its being contracted out to a private agency or agencies). A fee is charged for this service which ought to cover all the associated costs.[1]

Although the right levels of the vehicle excise duty cannot be so precisely quantified, there is a strong case for imposing this duty at significant rates in order to charge for some of the costs of private vehicles to the taxpayer that cannot be offset by the petrol duty.

As long as something like the present system of planning permission is retained, there is a case for imposing charges for at least certain categories of permission. This would introduce an element of market economics into what is at present a purely verbal and political struggle; it would also introduce more equality of arms between opponents of development, who have a free-rider problem, and developers, who have not.

(vi) Royalties and Licences as Alternatives to Income Taxation

Royalties and licences may on occasion be close substitutes for income taxation, especially in the business of mineral extraction.

The only example in Britain has been North Sea oil. The régime for the taxation of North Sea oil has been subject to numerous changes as the government has moved the goal posts to its own advantage year after year. It would have been fairer as well as more economic for the government to take its share 'up front' by auctioning licences to extract and then subjecting any resulting profits to the normal régime of corporation tax. This alternative was advocated while there was still an opportunity to put it into practice;[2] but nothing was done while there was time, and it is probably too late now.

(vii) Tax Relief and Opting Out

Paradoxical as it may seem, a tax relief may be an alternative to a charge for goods or services provided by the government: the tax relief covers only the taxpayer's marginal tax rate (thus accounting for less than 100 per cent of the cost of the good or service), and

---

[1] Immigration control is another hard-core government responsibility and one that might appear to offer little scope for charging. However, it has been reported that Suckling Airways hired immigration officers in Summer 1990 for its twice-daily service from Amsterdam to a small airport near Cambridge; this has allowed Suckling to establish itself outside London. The £21-an-hour charge is laid down in the Immigration Act 1988. The same report said that the Home Office was having talks with the British Airports Authority about introducing a general charge at this level for the services of immigration officers at Gatwick and Heathrow.

[2] Peter Lilley, MP, *North Sea Giveaway: The Case for Auctioning North Sea Oil Licences*, London: Bow Publications, 1980.

the balance which has to be provided by the taxpayer as a qualifying condition for entitlement to the relief may replace funds that would otherwise be provided by the government. Tax relief can thus reduce taxation and government spending simultaneously.

Tax relief also represents the devolutionary extreme of hypothecation. The initiative lies with the taxpayer, so that the volume of tax relief is demand-determined. The process of tax-relieving the expenditure concerned earmarks the tax that would have been collected but for the relief for the purpose for which the relief is granted. The whole operation has its own built-in checks and guarantees.

Health and education are areas of spending for which tax relief is particularly suitable.

(viii) Parafiscal Charges

Parafiscal charges are quasi-taxes with an element of in-built benefit-entitlement. They differ from royalties and licences as alternatives to income taxation in that the relationship between charge and benefit is not clear-cut (whereas the payment of a royalty or licence fee in substitution for income tax gives the taxpayer no more and no less than he would have had by paying a higher rate of tax on income; and the benefit from the tax reduction is also clear-cut, though for different reasons).

At one extreme, the benefits obtainable from the charge are so closely related to it that the charge has essentially the quality of a market price for services; at the other extreme, the relationship between the two is so remote or arcane that the charge is little, if anything, other than a general tax.

Over nearly 50 years since the publication of the Beveridge Report, National Insurance contributions have moved from somewhere near the former extreme to somewhere near the latter. We believe that policy should move in the opposite direction; welfare would be increased if parafiscal charges were more closely related to entitlement. Most of the items in Table 1 are commercially insurable for the majority of the population, provided that the State does not make itself a privileged competitor; for the minority of the population for whom this might be difficult or impossible, much of the present system could with advantage be replaced by State subsidisation of commercial insurance premiums. Beveridge argued that even unemployment insurance could be supplied in the market.

(ix) Compulsory Loans

British government expenditure during the Second World War was in part financed by a system of compulsory loans called post-war credits. They acquired a down-market image as a result of their loss in value through inflation during the lengthy period before their repayment; but an up-dated version of compulsory loans would have a number of advantages as a replacement for a tranche of taxes on saving, that is, taxes on income and capital.

Within the conceptual framework of the present paper, compulsory loans are a parafiscal charge whose proceeds are earmarked for their own eventual repayment. They conform closely to the benefit principle (since each taxpayer benefits from his own loan, after deduction of the inevitable handling charge); and the replacement of taxes with compulsory loans creates wealth through the voluntary principle (since the taxpayer's money is restored to him in the end and he retains a proprietory interest in it even during the interval). An increase in future government debt repayment might also serve to restrain the growth of government spending programmes over the medium term.

In order to make compulsory loans more acceptable to taxpayers, they could be repayable in stages and indexed against inflation.

Formal and Substantial Earmarking

The distinction between formal and substantial earmarking may also be described as the distinction between nominal and real earmarking. This distinction was mentioned at the end of Section 4 (above, page 56).

An extreme example of purely formal earmarking is the National Defence Contribution (above, page 71) which was not separately funded, was not equal to the total amount of the relevant expenditure, and did not determine or even influence the amount of that expenditure. However, even without separate funding and expenditure determination, a tax nominally earmarked for a particular form of spending may help to bring home to the public the true cost to them of goods and services 'free' at the point of consumption. Taxes with potential for this purpose include value added tax and, more particularly, income tax. The basic rate of income tax, for example, could be divided between the cost of supporting the NHS (in the previous year) and the rest. This might be a way of bringing home to the public the cost of demand-led expenditure such as various forms of welfare expenditure and elements of expenditure on the NHS. The identification and separation of an NHS element of income tax might help to make people understand just how much the NHS costs. Totals of NHS expenditure at the macro-economic level are frequently published; but they do not identify the cost to individual taxpayers at the micro-economic level, which could act as a discipline on demand. This is the flaw in the opinion polls on the subject.[1]

A more constructive proposal is the replacement of government spending by tax relief at similar cost. This has the advantage of reducing both government spending and taxation at little or no cost to the Treasury. An example is the proposal to replace child benefit by a child tax allowance of similar value to the taxpayer, the mother to retain the right to be paid in cash, as at present.[2]

Thus, although the more substantive types of earmarking would influence or even determine government spending for particular purposes in accordance with the amount of money raised for these purposes in taxation, there is in addition scope for more nominal forms of earmarking, either to bring home to the public the cost of government spending in certain forms or to reduce government spending and taxation simultaneously.

Control of Government Spending

Earmarking is a means of informing the taxpayer about what is going on; more importantly, it shifts power from the centre to the periphery and gives the taxpayer more control over his own destiny. It is thus complementary rather than alternative to an improved control over government spending.

The institutions affecting the control of government spending have been largely untouched by reform since the change of government in 1979. The only major reform has been the re-instatement of cash limits in current prices in place of the inflation-adjusted 'volume' figures which insulated government spending from the effects of rising prices. The 'Star Chamber' or Cabinet Committee charged with reconciling differences between the Treasury and the spending Departments has the job of resolving problems that originate elsewhere; it comes into action only partway through the annual spending round and cannot go to the root of problems at an early stage of the cycle.

The present system was not designed for government expenditure absorbing a third or two-fifths of Gross Domestic Product;

---

[1] Arthur Seldon, *Capitalism, op. cit.*, pp. 326-28.

[2] *Budget '90: A Low Tax Strategy*, Institute of Directors Representations for the 1990 Budget, London: IOD, 1990, para. 105.

nor would anybody starting from scratch come up with anything like the present system. Main faults are that expenditure is decided independently without the tax consequences being computed in parallel; that there is no zero-base budgeting, so that most items of expenditure, once included, are included for ever, irrespective of whether they are still needed; and that Ministers and civil servants advance their careers by spending taxpayers' money, not by economising.

The reform of the institutional framework of control over government spending is a topic beyond the scope of the present paper; but one suggestion can be made. At present, the incentive structure is all wrong; and this is where reform might best begin. New Zealand provides a precedent: as a result of a recent innovation, the Governor of the Bank of New Zealand now has a salary inversely related to the rate of inflation. Similarly, it could be made known at the highest level that the route to honours and preferment for British Ministers and officials lay through economy of government spending and not through additional expenditure.

SEVEN

Principles Underlying Reform

Purposes of Earmarking

The purposes of earmarking are to create wealth through the extension of pricing and adherence to the benefit principle of taxation; to create wealth through the use of the voluntary principle; to disseminate information and improve public understanding of how money is raised in taxation and how it is used; to influence the amounts of money spent by the government under particular headings; and to help to control the rise in aggregate government spending. Earmarking may also be useful as a temporary or transitional measure.

If earmarking influences the amounts spent under particular headings, the degree of influence may vary from negligibly small to total control.

Any serious attempt to make the tax system accountable to the individual taxpayer requires that the information presented to him should be simple and intelligible. This limits the options available and may call for institutional change.

Any form of earmarking shifts the balance of power away from the State and towards the individual. What are the arguments for and against such a shift in Britain?

State and Individual

Rationale of the present system

Although the idea of earmarking is familiar in Britain through particular examples over the years, it has not been actively canvassed as a principle of general application. The statist or establishment case for the present neglect of earmarking is in line with the traditional treatment of earmarking in the theory of public finance. The argument is that choices in public spending are made through a democratic process. Earmarking introduces compartments that reduce the efficiency of that process. There is little public pressure for change. On the contrary, opinion polls regularly indicate a wish for higher government spending on welfare services. Most people do not wish to be financially responsible for their pensions and their medical and educational requirements, and many are not competent to take on these responsibilities.

Criticisms of the present system

The critic's answer to this argument is that earmarking is an exercise in second best. It offers improvements on a system which is not ideal but deeply flawed. British governments often fail to obtain re-election, even though that is their principal policy objective; if they cannot effectively secure their own interests, how can they be more efficient in procuring the taxpayer's requirements than he would be himself? How can government look further ahead than the individual if its time-horizon is bounded by the next Election? Few firms would survive in business if they ran their finances as inefficiently as British governments run those of the nation: expenditure decisions are taken in advance and independently of income decisions, and there is no balance sheet and no proper distinction between income and capital. General government expenditure has been set to rise by 38 per cent over the three years 1988-89 to 1991-92 by a Government committed to economy. Political decisions are taken without consensus on the basis of a 51 per cent majority and may be reversed a few years later. Experience with the community charge indicates that, whatever they may tell pollsters, people are not keen to pay taxes when they are aware of doing so. Respondents tell pollsters that they accept higher taxes to obtain better welfare services only because the questioner does not offer them the option of paying for these services privately. The majority of people are not less competent than government to obtain efficient welfare services; in particular, parents have a street wisdom in the education of their children that the educational establishment has conspicuously lacked over the last generation or more. People in all walks of life have become responsible home-owners. Where people have had a chance to move away from the pocket-money economy, in which their major needs are provided by the State, they have done so. The European Community principle of subsidiarity (or maximum devolution) should be extended to welfare services in Britain.

The balance of the argument

The thesis of the present paper is that the deep-seated deficiencies of the existing system constitute a strong argument for reform and that it is not enough to defend the system as bearing any resemblance to the textbook ideals of the traditional theory of public finance. There is therefore a strong case in general for earmarking and devolution, even though the case is stronger in some areas than others.

Tax Reliefs, Vouchers and Loans

Tax reliefs are the ultimate form of devolved earmarking. The relief is conditional on the expenditure, taxpayer by taxpayer. The relief is always less than 100 per cent of the expenditure and usually much less than 50 per cent; with no personal tax being charged at more than 40 per cent in Britain, the relief would not be more than 40 per cent under the present system, and most income tax payers would enjoy relief only at the basic rate of 25 per cent. Since the tax relief is by definition a relief for expenditure considered worthy of government support, it serves to fund government spending on the cheap and is thus an economical use of public money. Even if some of the beneficiaries of tax relief are free-riders in the sense that they would have spent the same even without the tax relief, this is a normal ingredient of any price-cutting situation (not all customers buy more); and the fact that the expenditure is considered worthy of government support implies that the 'free-riders' have as much claim on this support as anyone else. The fact that the take-up of tax relief is voluntary (since the taxpayer has to make a claim) implies that tax relief may be a good means of advancing devolution in areas of policy (like welfare provision) where opinion is divided and there is no consensus.

By comparison with tax relief, government grants for the same purposes, in cash or in kind, have the disadvantage of increasing both government spending and taxation. They are administratively expensive, since the money goes round in a circle and comes back as grant to the same citizen who paid for it originally by way of taxation. However, grants provide access for non-taxpayers to government funds. Grants for specified purposes are earmarked government expenditure without a corresponding source of earmarked government funds; this again is a merit of tax reliefs over grants, since tax reliefs provide the earmarked expenditure and its funding in a single operation.

Training vouchers are already in use; variants of the voucher idea could be used in schooling, higher education, health care and housing. Vouchers are payments in kind for earmarked government spending; even if they are inferior to tax reliefs for the same purposes, they could be superior to the present system in which decisions are taken collectively on behalf of groups of consumers and the individual is deprived of the power of the purse.

Loans to students and others are forms of government spending that may prove to be temporary. If the loans are in cash, the expenditure is not effectively earmarked for its nominal purpose, since money is fungible and the loans may be used for something else. From the national standpoint, the repayment of the loan is most logically treated as negative expenditure (like privatisation receipts), even though from the standpoint of the individual concerned it has the quality of a tax and even of an earmarked tax.

EIGHT

Possible Innovations in Britain

This section notes areas of policy in which earmarking and related concepts might be applied in Britain. The topics mentioned are tax reliefs, vouchers, taxes, compulsory loans, parafiscal charges, planning permission, local government, charging, lotteries, charities, health provision and road funding. Some of the applications under taxes, local government and health are merely formal and presentational; but all the rest (as well as other applications under these headings) are substantial and affect what happens. Nothing is added here to what was said under 'Earmarking and other alternative medicines', above, about earmarking of spending by government departments, royalties and licences as alternatives to income taxation and the control of government spending. The comparison of tax revenues and related heads of government spending is the subject of *Whither Your Taxes?* by Gabriel Stein,[1] and these figures are not reported here.

Tax Reliefs

Tax reliefs are an integral part of the present system. *Inland Revenue Statistics 1990* lists 19 reliefs against income tax (at a total cost of £20,035 million, with double counting), *plus* 21 further reliefs against income tax/corporation tax of which the costs are not known, *plus* allowances and exemptions from income tax (costing respectively £28,385 million and £2,165 million), *plus* allowances, reliefs and exemptions from corporation tax, petroleum revenue tax, capital gains tax, inheritance tax and stamp duty. The total quantified cost was just over £81 billion in 1989-90 (inclusive of double counting), which was a little more than the net receipts of all Inland Revenue taxes in the same year (nearly £77 billion).

Tax relief for private medical insurance for those aged 60 or over was introduced in 1989 at a full-year cost of some £40 million. The government's accounts ignore the corresponding reduction in government spending; but, even when allowance is made for free riders, the saving in expenditure should be more than the nominal

---

[1] *IEA Inquiry 23*, London: IEA, 1991.

cost, since at 25 and 40 per cent rates of income tax the taxpayer has to pay out of his own pocket between one and a half and three times the amount he obtains in tax relief.

There is at present no corresponding tax relief for educational expenditure; but similar considerations apply.

The tax cost of the National Health Service was some £20 billion in 1989-90; the cost of local authority educational spending about £19 billion; the Department of Education's spending on higher education was over £3 billion. Thus the scope for economising on these figures through the use of tax reliefs is substantial, at least after a period of years. The Institute of Directors recently suggested tax reliefs costing initially £1 billion a year and rising thereafter;[1] and it may prove possible to improve on this materially.

The 1988 Finance Act disallowed claims for tax repayment by individuals receiving covenanted income. This was not a tax relief and had never been so treated by the Inland Revenue; it was the logical consequence of transferring income. A principal use of the system had been the financial support of students by their parents. A main effect of the change in 1988 was to preclude the use of personal allowances against income tax by students other than those with sufficient income from investments of their own. The restoration of what was a normal part of the system before 1988 would remove a distortion that at present increases the cost of privately purchased educational services.

Vouchers

Vouchers are an element of the Department of Employment's training programme; the IEA has long been interested in their use for the financing of primary and secondary education.[2] By comparison with tax reliefs, vouchers increase both taxation and government expenditure. But tax reliefs do not benefit non-taxpayers, and something else is required if they are to benefit as well. Vouchers (a form of payment in kind) are one possibility; direct payments, through the subsidisation of insurance premiums, are another.

Another rôle of vouchers is to provide a larger proportion of the market price than is provided by tax relief at 25 or 40 per cent; vouchers can provide up to 100 per cent and can thus secure a

[1] *Continuing Tax Reform: A Long Term Strategy for Government Spending and Taxation*, London: IOD, 1990, p. 122.

[2] In particular, A. K. Maynard, *Experiment with Choice in Education*, Hobart Paper 64, 1975; S. R. Dennison, *Choice in Education*, Hobart Paperback 19, 1984; Arthur Seldon, *The Riddle of the Voucher*, Hobart Paperback 21, 1986.

more level playing field between services paid for privately and services offered free at the point of consumption by the State. However, it is also possible to grant tax relief at more than the marginal rate of tax, so that the same result can be achieved through the tax system.[1]

Income Tax and Other Taxes

The best taxes to earmark are sectoral taxes or taxes levied at high rates or taxes which are perceived as personal levies by the individual taxpayer. From this standpoint, value added tax (VAT) is the least suitable tax for earmarking. On the other hand, the best taxes to earmark are those with an unlimited life expectancy, and not those which are candidates for early abolition or whose longer-term future is in doubt. From this standpoint, VAT is a more suitable tax for earmarking than almost any other. The tax system has been moving from an income base to an expenditure base for many years, and this process is more likely to be continued than reversed.[2] This implies a continuing reduction in taxes on income and capital by comparison with taxes on expenditure; indeed, it has recently been argued that over the next generation taxes on income and capital could be abolished, leaving expenditure as the only tax base.[3] Among expenditure taxes, excise duties are more likely to fall than to rise relatively to VAT, at least in Britain, whether through harmonisation within the European Community or through moves towards more fiscal neutrality between items subject to excise duties and other forms of consumers' expenditure. Thus VAT is the weakest candidate for earmarking in the short term, whereas in the long term it may have few rivals, if any.

This conflict is more apparent than real. Earmarking is an exercise in second best. If the tax system were to consist mostly or entirely of VAT on a broad base at a moderate, equiproportional rate, the case for earmarking would have disappeared along with the opportunity for its implementation. Meanwhile, earmarking has work to do.

It is arguable that much of the yield of *inheritance tax* ought to be earmarked for the upkeep of large houses and other heritage assets which inheritance tax prevents the family owners from maintaining

---

[1] The same point was made in the context of charitable giving in *The Wealth of Giving, op. cit.*, p. 79.

[2] John Kay, 'Routes to Fiscal Neutrality', in *Which Road to Fiscal Neutrality?*, IEA Readings No. 32, IEA, 1990.

[3] 'Continuing Tax Reform', *op. cit.*

themselves. But inheritance tax and *capital gains tax* have never attracted a consensus of support; they are not accepted taxes and they may have a short expectation of life. They also yield little revenue. Earmarking in these circumstances could do more harm than good.

By contrast, *income tax* is an important revenue raiser (£55 billion out of a total yield of £159 billion forecast for taxes and royalties, excluding national insurance contributions and the community charge, in 1990-91). It also has a substantial life expectancy, even if it can be abolished eventually. Moreover, self-employed people are required to make a return of income to the Inland Revenue by the autumn of each year and receive a tax assessment towards the end of the calendar year, and employees and pensioners receive at least a notice of coding (in January/February and/or April/May); there is thus a channel of communication already open from the Inland Revenue to most taxpayers.[1]

There are two main ways of earmarking income tax, one formal and one substantive. *Formally*, the Inland Revenue could provide information to the taxpayer once a year about the income-tax cost of government spending under various headings. For example, total net payments to European Community institutions were some £2,030 million in 1989-90 and planned to be £1,870 million in 1990-91, £1,670 million in 1991-92 and £1,990 million in 1992-93. The full-year yield of a penny point on the basic rate of income tax was put at £1,900 million for 1991-92 in Autumn 1989 and £2,175 million for 1992-93 in Autumn 1990. Information included with the notice of coding or otherwise could relate expected net payments to Community institutions to the yield of a penny on the basic rate: Community institutions currently cost slightly less than one penny point. This information would be much easier to understand than what is at present provided by local authorities for purposes of the community charge.

Another possible example is health spending out of tax revenue, which was put at £26,330 million in 1992-93 in the Autumn Statement 1990; this is rather more than 12 pence on the basic

---

[1] This channel of communication should be used to present each income earner and pensioner with whom the Revenue are in correspondence with an annual statement showing government expenditure on social security, health and education (together about half of total spending) and on all other items together. This information could be shown in millions of pounds; but it would probably be more useful to show it annually and weekly per head of population and for a family of four (two adults and two minor children). This last total is some £15,000 in 1990-91 (general government expenditure of £217·5 billion divided by a population of 57·35 million and multiplied by 4).

rate of income tax or nearly half the yield of the basic rate of 25 pence. Information like this, which is not widely understood at present, could contribute to a better informed public discussion of fiscal priorities. This earmarking would be formal in the sense that it would not affect the outcome; but it could be given added point if a formally separate Health Tax were taken out of income tax and given an identity of its own. Thus the Chancellor could announce at budget time that the rate of health tax required to pay for expected health expenditure during the coming year would be (say) 12·1 pence, and income tax would be (say) 12·9 pence, giving a basic rate of income and health tax of 25 pence.

It would also be possible to earmark a health tax *substantively*; health spending in a financial year might be limited to the proceeds of (say) a 12 pence Health Tax announced at the start of that year. This would conform with the principle (commonplace outside government) that income determines expenditure and not the other way round.

An alternative approach to health taxation is discussed below. *Excise duties* are discussed under road taxation.

It is strongly arguable that taxation is not the most effective means of controlling pollution and is inferior, in particular, to market-based regulation. If use is made of *pollution taxes*, however, their yield might suitably be earmarked for the control of pollution and the compensation of its victims.

Parafiscal Charges

Most forms of social security provision could be turned into funded private-sector insurance, at least if a measure of government financial support were provided for the insured; as the Appendix (below, page 101) shows, a number of social security arrangements originated in private-sector insurance through friendly societies. This includes unemployment benefit.[1]

The attraction of the present pay-as-you-go system when it was introduced was that it gave a whole generation of beneficiaries something for nothing. Much of that generation is now dead, and the benefits enjoyed without payment are beyond recall. A move back to funded insurance would for similar reasons require a whole generation to pay twice. That and the attraction for government of some £40 billion of parafiscal revenue which can be used as though it were tax revenue account for a certain reluctance to

---

[1] Tim Evans, *A Friend in Need*, London: Adam Smith Institute, 1990.

change. This has been one of the areas of policy where progress towards privatisation since 1979 has been most glacial.

Eppur si muove: There has been progress nevertheless. The move into personal pensions from SERPS (the state earnings-related pension scheme) induced by measures brought in in 1988[1] attracted such interest that the government was several billions of pounds out of pocket at the end of 1989-90 by comparison with the original estimates.[2] But this was not a zero-sum loss, in which the government lost what contributors gained. On the contrary, the whole purpose of the 1988 provisions was to exploit an overlap of interest between the government and the contributor; the government lost in the short term only because the contributor (who could not benefit unless he took the initiative) exploited this overlap more vigorously than had been expected. So what is the nature of this overlap?

The Government was concerned that its obligations under SERPS were building up so rapidly that they would be insupportable in a generation or so as a result of demographic trends. It therefore tried to unload these obligations onto a community of contributors who were assumed to be more interested in reducing year-by-year contributions than in the eventual return from staying with the pay-as-you-go system. The Government was not expecting to lose. In theory, there would be a trade-off between a more far-sighted government, with a lower rate for discounting the future, and a more near-sighted community of contributors, with a higher rate for discounting the future and a more focussed interest in the outcome of the next few years. This is pretty rich, given that the government runs its accounts and takes its decisions on a year-by-year basis, as no public company could afford to do, whereas the humblest citizen is accustomed to taking out life assurance, pension or mortgage obligations reaching for up to 30 years or more into the future. This reversal of rôles requires another explanation.

Reasons for opting out
It is not enough to say that the public's rate of discount turned out to be even further above the Government's than the

---

[1] The incentive to opt out of SERPS was a rebate of 5·8 per cent of national-insurance-relevant earnings plus a bonus of 2 per cent of these earnings. This could amount to as much as £1,340 a year for three years, or a maximum of £4,020.

[2] According to a report published by the National Audit Office in December 1990, the National Insurance Fund is likely to lose a cumulative sum of at least £9·3 billion by the end of the option in 1993 as compared with an eventual saving in lower pensions of £3·4 billion; the disproportion is even larger when the latter figure is discounted back to its present value.

Government had expected, although this may have accounted for a substantial proportion of the overrun in demand. What seems to have happened is that another dimension came into play. The larger-than-predicted number of contributors who opted out of SERPS could have been motivated by a mixture of two considerations. First, there was an element of ownership or control available in any alternative to a state-funded pay-as-you-go scheme so that astute management could improve the returns from the funds invested. Secondly, as long as entitlements are unfunded, they are politically at risk. The Government in power during the 1980s has drastically devalued the contributory principle, in particular by removing the ceiling on employers' contributions (apparently in response to a short-term shortage of funds just before a Budget). If government can increase contributions in response to short-term pressures, it can reduce benefits for the same reason. If demographic pressures are severe during the early decades of the next century, an easy target for economy would be the state retirement pensions payable to the 'rich' (perhaps the highest quarter or third of incomes). They would have no redress.

With the benefit of hindsight, the Government could have attracted the custom it wanted on less generous terms. But this is only another way of saying that the Government had underestimated the demand for the alternative it was offering and thus the extent of the overlap of interest between State and contributor that this alternative represented. If government's book-keeping included a capital account, like the books of any company, the overlap of interest between government and contributor would be still more extensive. The government would be reducing its short-term income but also reducing its long-term liabilities. The loss of short-term income could therefore prudently be funded by government borrowing, which would enlarge the scope for incentives to the contributor without imposing additional burdens on the taxpayer.

The reform of the government's accounts, from the present cash-flow basis to commercial income-and-capital book-keeping, is the solution to the problem of one generation paying twice when pay-as-you-go funding of state retirement pensions is replaced, in whole or in part, by commercial funding from investments. The shortfall in government income caused by the replacement of national insurance contributions with contributions to commercial insurance funds can properly be met, at least in large measure, by additional government short-term borrowing corresponding to reduced government long-term liabilities, as a capital account would show.

Commercial insurance is an ultimate form of earmarking, since contributions are earmarked pound by pound for each contributor in accordance with the terms of his policy. Genuine funding would replace the present spurious National Insurance Fund.

Similar principles apply to most forms of social security benefit. Wealth is created by the extension of the voluntary principle, of which the contributory principle is an important part. Most of the risks covered by social security are insurable, the major exception being elements of poverty. Privatisation would promote competition and enable the contributor to get a better deal by shopping around. The massive expenditure of the Department of Social Security (planned at over £58 billion in 1991-92) would be targeted more economically if much of it were used to subsidise or tax-relieve commercial insurance premiums, in so far as might be necessary or desirable.

Health Care

Mention was made earlier of the possibility of dedicating an element of income tax, formally or substantively, to the defrayal of government expenditure on health care. There are a number of other possible forms of earmarking for medical expenditure.

The simplest form of earmarking is an extension of the tax relief for private medical insurance first introduced in 1989 for the insurance of those aged 60 or over. Tax relief is a precisely targeted form of earmarking and the matching principle ensures an economical use of tax revenue forgone.

A recent report notes that tax funding in the UK has failed to deliver the volume of resources needed to finance services to the level demanded by the public and that expenditure in the UK is still lower than would be expected by international comparisons.[1] This finding is consistent with the thesis of the present paper that earmarking liberates additional funds for spending on the purposes concerned because most people are more willing to part with money as consumers than as taxpayers.

In *A New Deal for Health Care*,[2] Sir Leon Brittan proposes that employees' national insurance contributions should be set at the level required to fund the National Health Service; the shortfall in national insurance contributions for the funding of social security benefits would be made good from taxation. Thus a tranche of

---

[1] Chris Ham, Ray Robinson and Michaela Benzeval, *Health Check: Health Care Reforms in an International Context*, London: King's Fund Institute, 1990, p. 95.

[2] London: Conservative Political Centre, 1988.

IEA PUBLICATIONS
Subscription Service

An annual subscription is the most convenient way to obtain our publications. Every title we produce in all our regular series will be sent to you immediately on publication and without further charge, representing a substantial saving.

Individual subscription rates*

Britain: £30·00 p.a. including postage.
£28·00 p.a. if paid by Banker's Order.
£18·00 p.a. to teachers and students who pay *personally*.

Europe: £30·00 p.a. including postage.

South America: £40·00 p.a. or equivalent.

Other Countries: Rates on application. In most countries subscriptions are handled by local agents. Addresses are available from the IEA.

* These rates are *not* available to companies or to institutions.

To: The Treasurer, Institute of Economic Affairs,
2 Lord North Street, Westminster,
London SW1P 3LB

I should like to subscribe from ....

I enclose a cheque/postal order for:

☐ £30·00

☐ £18·00   I am a teacher/student at ....

....

☐ Please send a Banker's Order form.

☐ Please send an invoice.

☐ Please charge my credit card:

Please tick   ☐ VISA   ☐ ▲   ☐ AMERICAN EXPRESS   ☐ ⓓ

Card No: ☐☐☐☐☐☐☐☐☐☐☐☐☐☐☐☐☐☐

In addition I would like to purchase the following previously published titles:

....

....

Name ....

Address ....   ⎫
                                                                        ⎬ BLOCK
         ....   ⎪ LETTERS
                                                                        ⎪ PLEASE
         .... Post Code .... ⎭

Signed .... Date ....

RM46

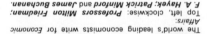

income tax would pay for social security benefits instead of the NHS and a tranche of national insurance contributions would pay for the NHS instead of social security benefits. The change would be formal rather than substantive (in particular, the cost of the NHS would determine the level of National Health Insurance contributions); but, like the foregoing proposal for an element of income tax dedicated to the NHS, it would serve to bring home the cost of the NHS to a much larger number of people.

Any of these ideas could be combined with an extension of charging in the NHS, notably through the institution of hotel charges in hospitals.[1]

The argument of the present paper indicates that tax relief is the option to be preferred, since the take-up is voluntary and it reduces both taxation and government spending. If tax relief at the basic rate of income tax (currently 25 per cent) is inadequate to elicit the response desired from basic-rate taxpayers, the rate of tax relief could be increased above their marginal rate of tax, for example to 40 per cent, the excess to be available for offset against tax on other income but not to give entitlement to repayment in cash.[2] The next best option is a voucher or other entitlement empowering the patient to take his custom to the practice, consultant or hospital that provides him with the best service.

Education

Tax relief for private expenditure on education would be a form of earmarking with advantages similar to those of tax relief for private expenditure on medical insurance.

Corporation Tax Losses

The present arcane and archaic restrictions on the use of corporation tax losses (particularly when a change of ownership is combined with an alleged change in the nature of a trade or business) are a major obstacle to commercial efficiency and survival.[3] The removal of these restrictions would make the tax system more neutral between taxpayer and tax authorities and would be better targeted than perhaps any other reform for promoting business efficiency and avoiding business failures.

---

[1] A wide range of options compatible with the extension of consumer choice is discussed in David Green *et al.*, *The NHS Reforms: Whatever Happened to Consumer Choice?*, IEA Health and Welfare Unit Health Series No. 11, November 1990.

[2] *The Wealth of Giving, op. cit.*, pp. 41, 79.

[3] Barry Bracewell-Milnes, *A Market in Corporation Tax Losses*, London: Institute of Directors, 1983.

Corporation tax has been among the most buoyant taxes recently in times of expansion; an element of corporation tax could be earmarked for defraying the cost of removing restrictions on the use of corporation tax losses.

Compulsory Loans

The replacement of inheritance tax and capital gains tax with compulsory loans of the same amount would be an improvement on the present system; but it would run the risk of distracting attention from the more important task of reforming or abolishing these taxes.

Planning Permission

The sale or auctioning of planning permissions has long been of interest to the IEA.[1] The system has been moving in this direction informally, since developers often offer or are required to undertake infrastructural expenditure as the price of obtaining planning permission. But the resulting price mechanism is highly imperfect and, at least for large or controversial developments, more formal arrangements might work much more efficiently.

One element of the charge for planning permission would be earmarked for infrastructural spending. Another element might be earmarked for the compensation of losers from the development. Charges for planning permission might be used to fund the additional compensation of home-owners for which provision is made in the Planning and Compensation Bill published in November 1990; previously residents received the market value of their house calculated on the basis that the development was not happening, together with moving costs and a home loss payment of up to £1,500. Another possibility is that objectors to small-scale but controversial developments might be able to outbid the developer in the purchase of development rights which they had no intention of using: up to the level of the failed bid, the charge for this 'planning permission' could be used to compensate the thwarted developer, provided that developments could be excluded if their main purpose was to attract money from this quarter.

Local Government

If local government is to be made financially accountable to its electors, the community charge must cease to be opaque and become transparent. Ideally, local authority expenditure would be

---

[1] F. G. Pennance, *Housing, Town Planning and the Land Commission*, Hobart Paper 40, IEA, 1967.

financed entirely by the community charge and the community charge would be earmarked entirely for the financing of local authority expenditure.

The reform of local government financing is a topic beyond the scope of the present paper; but two general lines of reform may be suggested. The first is that the present system of precepting for the educational and other expenditure of county councils should come to an end (whether through the abolition of county councils, the centralisation or privatisation of educational expenditure, direct billing by county councils or otherwise); the authority determining the level of the community charge would then be the same as the authority spending its proceeds.[1] The second is that there should be a clearer distinction between discretionary spending of local authorities (funded by the community charge) and other spending (funded by central government, whether through the national non-domestic rate or otherwise).

Charging

Charging (of which commercial insurance premiums are an important example) is the ultimate form of earmarking: a pooled tax is transformed into an individual's payment for a service rendered to the same individual.

Arthur Seldon in *Charge*[2] classified government spending in 1974 as follows:

	Per cent
Charging impracticable or uneconomic	15
Charging partly practicable	14
Charging substantially practicable	40
Disbursements mostly in cash	22
Interest on National Debt	9
	100

---

[1] The confusion between the functions of the borough (collecting 100 per cent of the rates or community charge) and those of the county council (spending the majority of the proceeds) has had a parallel on a smaller scale in the confusion between the functions of local water concerns (obliged to precept for the sewerage charges of the regional water authority) and those of the regional water authority (spending the yield of the precept). Now that water has been privatised, at least one local water concern has lost little time in shedding the burden of the precept: 'Until now, Sutton District Water has acted as our agents, billing and collecting charges on our behalf. Unfortunately, Sutton District Water are unable to continue this service because of their charging policy.' (Circular of December 1990 from Thames Water Utilities.) Good for Sutton!

[2] *Op. cit.*, Table B, pp. 46-47.

Thus 54 per cent of total government spending could be charged for, wholly or in part. In addition, the present paper argues that a large proportion of cash payments can be replaced by insurance premiums, if necessary subsidised or tax-relieved by the government. Thus on these figures some three-quarters of government spending could be charged for, in whole or in part.

Progress since 1974 has not been dramatic. In *Charging for Public Services: A Paradigm for Empirical Analysis*,[1] Professor Richard Rose estimates that charges currently account for some £9 billion of government income or less than 5 per cent of expenditure.

'The pattern shown cannot be explained by prescriptive theories of market efficiency or merit goods, as an effort to obtain signals independent of revenue or by party differences: the pattern must be understood as an historical inheritance.'

As a simple example of what might be done but is not, a number of government-funded museums in the United Kingdom are in financial difficulties and some, like the Victoria and Albert Museum, have made highly qualified scholars redundant as a measure of economy. Little has been done to divide the market between customers with more time than money and customers with more money than time. Subscription membership giving entitlement to access in the evenings might pay for itself handsomely by attracting interest from people too busy to go in the daytime or at weekends. This could be combined with cheaper or free access at other times and might well raise additional funds for a wide range of museums, art galleries and libraries.

Lotteries

The United Kingdom has a long history of lotteries for public purposes including repairing the harbours of the Cinque Ports in 1566, the building of an aqueduct in London in the 17th century, and the building of the British Museum. The Irish Hospitals' Sweepstake was popular in the 1930s, although support for it was unlawful.[2]

As a consequence of the introduction of the Single European Market in 1992, the British government may be obliged to allow foreign operators to sell tickets for their national lotteries in Britain. The confiscation of letters from European lottery firms trying to sell tickets illegally in Britain has recently been running at about four million a year.

---

[1] Centre for the Study of Public Policy, University of Strathclyde, 1989.

[2] 'Lessons of the Lottery' (leading article), *Daily Telegraph*, 3 March 1990.

National and local government lotteries are a niche market for raising funds less painfully than through taxation. To avoid the greater evil of subsidised state competition with private business, the odds should be significantly less attractive than the best possible in the private sector after allowance for taxation. Given the element of perceived public service in participation in charitable lotteries, this should constitute no effective constraint.

Historical precedents and the contemporary evidence of charitable lotteries in Britain and government lotteries abroad suggest that there are virtually no limits to the range of causes which government lotteries might be enlisted to support. The arts, sports, environmental causes and capital expenditure on the National Health Service are among the more obvious candidates.[1]

Charitable Giving

The superiority of charitable giving over taxation as a means of raising funds for the same or similar purposes is a main theme of *The Wealth of Giving*.[2] By comparison with taxation, charitable giving creates wealth through the voluntary principle.

The traditional purposes of charity were mainly education, the care of the sick and the relief of poverty. Charitable activity is much wider now and includes animal welfare, the support of the arts, the preservation of the national heritage, environmental and green causes, and overseas aid. Charities could replace government activity in a number of these areas: for example, the wasteful business of government-to-government overseas aid could be replaced in part with assistance to small-scale private enterprise through intermediate technology.

Charities enjoy numerous tax privileges and there are few voices, if any, arguing that these privileges should be curtailed for charities in general. On the contrary, the debate is rather about whether these privileges should be extended.[3] Tax relief for charitable giving earmarks the tax revenue forgone for purposes of acknowledged

---

[1] A national lottery for the support of the arts was recommended by Denis Vaughan, *The Case for a National Arts Lottery*, London: Adam Smith Institute, 1990. A national lottery for the support of the arts, sport and the environment was proposed by Lord Birkett and debated in the House of Lords on 28 February 1990 (*Hansard*, cols. 776-804).

[2] *Op. cit.*

[3] Proposals for further reliefs or tax reductions are made in *Giving: How to Encourage Charities More*, Centre for Policy Studies, 1990. Other proposals are made in *The Wealth of Giving, op. cit.*, pp. 40-41, 78-79, in particular that the rate of tax relief for charitable giving could be above the taxpayer's marginal rate of tax if he has sufficient income or other taxable matter to absorb the excess.

public interest and attracts government money only on the matching principle that the government's contribution is proportional to that of the taxpayers; the matching principle is a self-regulating mechanism for testing the sincerity of the public concern.

Roads

As is explained in *Whither your Taxes?*, public sector revenue from the road taxes excluding driving licences, VAT and import duties was of the order of £13·2 billion in 1989-90. Total Department of Transport expenditure on transport and communications was some £5·8 billion in the same year.

A main change since the days of the Road Fund is that traffic congestion, shortages of parking space, pollution and the damage done to the environment by new roads are much more important considerations now. Transport policy and its financing are more complicated than they were, and it could now be simplistic to dedicate the yield of one or more road taxes to the building and maintenance of new roads.

There is nevertheless evidence both from the history of the Road Fund in Britain and from the acceptance of Proposition 111 (a vote to double the tax on petrol at the pump) in California in June 1990 that voters and taxpayers approve of a relationship between road taxes and expenditure on transport. Proposition 111 specifies that the additional money must be spent on improving California's public transport and road network.

There is thus a case for substantive earmarking of an element of road taxation for government expenditure on public transport. The details are beyond the scope of the present paper; but sources of funds might include fees for driving licences and for driving tests, car tax, vehicle licences, petrol duty and VAT on petrol, parking fees, parking fines, road tolls[1] and (in years to come) congestion taxes (in the form of permits or metered charges). Uses, in addition to new roads, might include the funding of driving tests, improvements in road maintenance, out-of-town parking provision, capital expenditure on railways and underground, traffic engineering and minor works to improve the usefulness of existing roads, and enhanced compensation for those losing financially from road building.

---

[1] Trafalgar House's Dartford Bridge is partly financed by tolls from the existing Dartford Tunnel. This illustrates how tolls can be used to expand the scope for the private funding of new roads, which is seriously underexploited at present: Treasury rules enable state-financed roadbuilding to compete with privately financed roadbuilding on terms which ignore the additional risks borne by the latter.

Fines

For most people in Britain, parking fines are the only fines they are ever likely to have to pay under threat of criminal proceedings. But the State's financial gains from more serious offences may also be recycled into the control of the offending activity.

It was reported in November 1990[1] that police and Customs were to be allowed to use cash seized from drug traffickers to fund operations against the trade. The Treasury, which had long argued that Britain's share of money from international operations should go to the Exchequer, had agreed that the first £20 million each year should be used for enforcement.

There is wide scope for the extension of this principle to payments both to public bodies and to individuals: the sharp boundary between civil and criminal law has been softened in recent years, and certain victims of criminal offences already receive a measure of restitution from public funds. The potential advantages of earmarking in this area of policy go beyond public finance to the principles of crime and its punishment.

Environmental Taxes

'Environmental taxes, like other market-based instruments, offer the potential for reducing pollution at lower cost than regulatory policies with equivalent effect.'

'The additional revenue would then be available to ameliorate some of the adverse effects—on industrial profitability (through reductions in other company taxes), on prices (through reductions in other indirect taxes) or on the standards of living of particular income groups (through offsetting changes in income tax and social security).'[2]

At one level this is a revenue-neutral change in the tax system and as such is open to the objection that the losers feel the losses more keenly than the gainers feel the gains. However, if new taxes are introduced for explicitly environmental purposes, their hypothecation for the reduction of other taxes may serve to prevent their simply resulting in an increase in the burden of aggregate taxation and government spending, as would happen if they were used to fund government spending on the environment.

---

[1] Neil Darbyshire and Michael Kerr in the *Daily Telegraph*, 8 November 1990.

[2] Steve McKay, Mark Pearson and Stephen Smith, 'Fiscal Instruments in Environmental Policy', *Fiscal Studies*, November 1990, p. 1.

NINE

Conclusion

This paper has argued that the traditional objections to earmarking are weak or invalid because they assume a Utopian system of public finance and democratic decision-taking that bears little or no relation to reality. Earmarking is an exercise in the second best or least bad: in an imperfect world, it can provide better decisions and do less damage to the creation of wealth than conventional pooled financing of government expenditures.

Earmarking creates wealth in two separate ways: by improving the allocation of resources and by giving scope to the voluntary principle. In each of these ways wealth is created through the replacement of compulsion by choice.

Tax relief represents the ultimate form of earmarking and also its devolutionary extreme: the tax otherwise payable is used to fund an activity which the government wishes to promote and the whole operation is voluntary, since it relies on the taxpayer's taking the initiative. It is also good value for money from the government's standpoint since the taxpayer pays out much more than he receives in tax relief, often well over twice as much.

There is also a range of other forms of earmarking, some formal, some substantive and some a mixture of the two. Income tax and national insurance contributions are the major taxes that appear to offer most potential for earmarking.

Earmarking is in its turn one of a range of methods of financing government expenditure otherwise than by the pooling of tax revenues. Charging, lotteries and the replacement of taxation with charitable giving, for example, are all means of reducing the loss of welfare and the weakening of incentives inherent in the financing of government expenditure from pooled taxation.

Although earmarking may be inferior to the outright privatisation of government expenditures and their return to the market economy, it can represent both a first step towards privatisation and an improvement in efficiency for as long as the activity in question remains a financial responsibility of government.

Social Insurance Funds

National Health Insurance

A National Health Insurance Fund was set up under section 54 of the National Insurance Act 1911, to receive contributions (section 3) by insured persons, employers and the Treasury and monies provided by Parliament to defray the corresponding benefits. The scheme covered employed persons who were members of approved societies (such as friendly societies and insurance companies) as well as non-members. The system contained an element of pay-as-you-go from the start, since members entering at more than the minimum starting age were entitled to full benefits; a levy on all contributions was credited to 'reserve values' provided to cover the liabilities so arising. Any surpluses were to be invested through the National Debt Commissioners.

The Central Fund was set up under section 4 of the National Health Insurance Act 1918, to strengthen the financial position of the weaker approved societies by diverting a portion of the sums retained out of the weekly contributions for the redemption of reserve values.

Unemployment Fund

An Unemployment Fund was set up under section 92 of the National Insurance Act 1911. The arrangements were similar to those for national health insurance, the role of 'approved societies' being taken here by 'associations of workmen in an insured trade'.

Widows', orphans' and old age contributory pensions

The Widows', Orphans' and Old Age Contributory Pensions Act 1936, superseding Acts with the same name of 1925 and 1929, set up a Pensions Account and a Treasury Pensions Account (section 14), the latter to receive any sums not required by the former to meet expenditure. Non-contributory pensions payable under the Old Age Pensions Act 1936 (consolidating earlier enactments) were payable out of monies voted by Parliament and had no fund or account of their own.

National Insurance: amalgamation of funds

Under section 66 of the 10th schedule of the National Insurance Act 1946, a National Insurance Fund and a National Insurance (Reserve) Fund were set up to acquire respectively the revenue and capital assets of the Unemployment Fund; three National Health Insurance Funds; the Central Fund; two other health insurance funds; and six pensions accounts under the Widows', Orphans' and Old Age Contributory Pensions Act 1936 and the Widows', Orphans' and Old Age Contributory Pensions (Voluntary Contributors) Act 1937.

Industrial injuries

The National Insurance (Industrial Injuries) Act 1946 set up an Industrial Injuries Fund (section 58), subject to the surveillance of the Government Actuary. This was merged with the National Insurance Fund in 1975.

Redundancy payments

The Redundancy Payments Act 1965 set up a Redundancy Fund (Part II, sections 26-36), funded by contributions from employers. These contributions were renamed 'employment protection allocations' (EPAs) by Schedule 16, paragraph 13, of the Employment Protection Act 1975. Cm. 948[1] (para. 8) announced the Government's intention to introduce legislation to combine the Redundancy Fund with the National Insurance Fund.

Maternity pay

The Employment Protection Act 1975 set up a Maternity Fund (sections 39 and 40) to be funded along the lines of the Redundancy Fund. A proportion of the employment protection allocations (EPAs) was allocated to the Maternity Fund. The fund was abolished by section 49 and Schedule 4, Part III, of the Social Security Act 1986.

National health contributions

National health contributions were an integral part of the National Insurance Act 1911. Rates of contributions for employers and employees were specified in the Second Schedule to the Act. They have been levied ever since. The weekly rates of contribution for

---

[1] *The Report of the Government Actuary on the Draft of the Social Security Benefits Uprating Order 1990 and the Social Security (Contributions) (Rerating) Order 1990,* Cm. 948, London: HMSO, 1990, para. 8.

1942 noted in the Beveridge Report[1] were 5.5d for employers and 5.5d for male and 5d for female employees.

The amalgamation of the National Health Insurance Funds into the National Insurance Funds in 1946, noted above, preceded the establishment of the National Health Service. When the NHS was set up, it received contributions from the National Insurance Fund; but it was not until the National Health Service Contributions Act of 1957 that a system of NHS contributions was formalised. The First Schedule to the Act imposed NHS contributions of 1s 4.5d a week on employed men, 1s 0.5d on employed women and 3.5d on employers. The corresponding rates in 1989-90 and 1990-91 are 1·05 per cent for employees and 0·9 per cent for employers of earnings within the band of Class 1 liability.

The amounts raised by NHS contributions are substantial. 'In 1989-90 it is estimated that over 78 per cent of the gross cost of the NHS in Great Britain will be met by general taxation and a little over 16 per cent by the NHS contribution.' (The remaining 6 per cent represents charges, land sales and miscellaneous sources of income.) 'Gross expenditure in 1989-90 in the NHS will be an estimated £21·2 billion.'[2] Sixteen per cent of £21·2 billion is some £3·4 billion or more than 1·5 pence on the basic rate of income tax. National Health Service contributions for Great Britain in 1990-91 are estimated in Appendix 6 of Cm. 948[3] at £4,120 million.

---

[1] *Social Insurance and Allied Services*, Cmd. 6404, London: HMSO, 1942, p. 227.

[2] *The Government's Expenditure Plans 1990-91 to 1992-93*, Cm. 1013, London: HM Treasury, January 1990, p. 6.

[3] *Op. cit.*

OF RELATED INTEREST

The Wealth of Giving
Every One in His Inheritance
BARRY BRACEWELL-MILNES

Charity is regarded by many as the antithesis of the market economy. The State is seen as having an important role in redirecting wealth to those less fortunate. Most economists accept that this involves a trade-off—government-induced re-distributions of wealth impair the incentives for wealth creation. In *The Wealth of Giving* another 'cost' is identified. It advances the thesis that the act of giving by individuals, families and institutions itself creates wealth. A gift is a source of utility for the donor and a financial gain to the recipient. Collective charity and the taxation of inheritance destroys this wealth, and imposes a real loss which cannot be captured by the tax collector or recipients of government expenditure.

The Wealth of Giving is a powerful analysis of the economics of giving and inheritance. It examines the different types of giving and the implications of social policies designed to tax private charity and inheritance. Dr Bracewell-Milnes, a Senior Research Fellow of the IEA, goes beyond theory to provide estimates of the gains and losses of different policies. His conclusions will be of interest to all those concerned about social policy and the interplay between government and the market in the provision of charity and gifts.

ISBN 0-255 36225-0   ***Research Monograph 43***   **£6·00**

THE INSTITUTE OF ECONOMIC AFFAIRS
2 Lord North Street, Westminster
London SW1P 3LB   Telephone: 071-799 3745